THE PRAYERS OF JESUS

Other works by the same author
Published by Fortress Press

The Eucharistic Words of Jesus
Jerusalem in the Time of Jesus
The Lord's Prayer
The Problem of the Historical Jesus
The Sermon on the Mount

JOACHIM JEREMIAS

The Prayers of Jesus

FORTRESS PRESS
Philadelphia

Chapters I and IV translated by John Bowden, and Chapter II by Dr. Christoph Burchard in Göttingen, from the German *Abba. Studien zur neutestamentlichen Theologie und Zeitgeschichte* (Vandenhoeck und Ruprecht, Göttingen 1966), pp. 15-67 ("Abba"), 67-80 ("Das tägliche Gebet im Leben Jesu und in der ältesten Kirche"), 145-52 ("Kennzeichen der *ipsissima vox Jesu*").

Chapter III, with some revision, from *The Lord's Prayer,* Facet Books, Biblical Series, 8, translated by John Reumann (Philadelphia: Fortress Press, 1964) (German original: *Das Vater-Unser im Lichte der neueren Forschung,* Calwer Hefte 50, Stuttgart, Calwer Verlag, 1962 = [4]1967, also in *Abba,* pp. 152-171).

Biblical quotations from the Revised Standard Version of the Bible, copyright 1946, 1952, © 1971, 1973 by the Division of Christian Education of the National Council of the Churches of Christ in the U.S.A., are used by permission.

First published in English in this edition 1967
First Fortress Press Edition 1978

Library of Congress Cataloging in Publication Data

Jeremias, Joachim, 1900-
  The prayers of Jesus.

  Translation of 2 works: chapter 1-2 and 4, selections from Abba; chapter 3, translation of Das Vater-unser im Lichte der Neueren Forschung.
  Includes indexes.
  1. Jesus Christ—Prayers. I. Title. II. Title: Jeremias, Joachim, 1900- Das Vater-unser im Lichte der Neueren Forschung. English. 1978.
BV229.J4 1978   232.9'5   77-10427
ISBN 0-8006-1322-8

CONTENTS

5

PREFACE

A LARGE collection of articles by Professor Jeremias was published by Vandenhoeck and Ruprecht in 1966 under the title *Abba. Studien zur neutestamentlichen Theologie und Zeitgeschichte.* As well as older work, it contained two fresh studies, one of them of considerable length. For various reasons, it has proved impracticable to translate the volume as it stands, and in any case some of its contents are at present readily available in English versions elsewhere. It did, however, seem important to make available as soon as possible the two hitherto unpublished studies and two others, which have a related theme and are of more than purely specialist interest. A further selection from *Abba*, to include more recent work by Professor Jeremias published after the German volume, is planned for a later date.

Passages from 'Abba', the first article, have appeared in condensed form in *The Central Message of the New Testament* (SCM and Scribner's, 1965), but the present book is offered to a rather different audience, and in any case provides an immense amount of documentation and specific comment which was out of place in the earlier work. The four articles of this volume overlap in a few places; this was not altered so as to keep each article readable by itself. The final study partly goes beyond the scope of the collection, but as 'Characteristics of the *ipsissima vox Jesu*' has become something of a classic of New Testament scholarship, it seemed a pity to omit it.

The translations come from three different hands, but they have all been supervised by Professor Jeremias and his assistant, Dr Christoph Burchard, with their usual meticulous care. Dr Burchard himself made the translation of the second article.

ABBREVIATIONS

BFCT	Beiträge zur Förderung christlicher Theologie, Gütersloh
Billerbeck	H. L. Strack-P. Billerbeck, *Kommentar zum Neuen Testament aus Talmud und Midrasch*, Munich, I 1922, II 1924, III 1926, IV 1928, V 1956, VI 1961
BJRL	*Bulletin of the John Rylands Library*, Manchester
Blass-Debrunner-Funk	F. Blass-A. Debrunner, *A Greek Grammar of the New Testament and other Early Christian Literature*. A Translation and Revision of the ninth-tenth German edition by R. W. Funk, London-Chicago 1961
Charles	R. H. Charles (ed.), *The Apocrypha and Pseudepigrapha of the Old Testament in English*, Oxford 1913; reissued 1963
ET	English Translation
FRLANT	Forschungen zur Religion und Literatur des Alten und Neuen Testaments, Göttingen
HUCA	Hebrew Union College Annual, Cincinnati, Ohio
HNT	Handbuch zum Neuen Testament, Tübingen
JBL	*Journal of Biblical Literature*, Philadelphia, Pa.
JQR	*The Jewish Quarterly Review*, Philadelphia, Pa.
NGG	*Nachrichten der Gesellschaft der Wissenschaften zu Göttingen*
NovT	*Novum Testamentum*, Leiden
NTD	Das Neue Testament Deutsch, Göttingen
NTS	*New Testament Studies*, Cambridge
PG	J. P. Migne, *Patrologiae cursus completus, Series Graeca*, Paris
RGG	*Die Religion in Geschichte und Gegenwart*, Tübingen
RHPR	*Revue d'Histoire et de Philosophie Religieuses*, Paris
SUNT	Studien zur Umwelt des Neuen Testaments, Göttingen

TLZ   *Theologische Literaturzeitung*, Berlin

TWNT   G. Kittel (ed.), *Theologisches Wörterbuch zum Neuen Testament*, Stuttgart, 1933ff. (The English version now being prepared and translated by G. W. Bromiley, Grand Rapids, Mich. 1964ff., has virtually the same pagination)

WUNT   Wissenschaftliche Untersuchungen zum Neuen Testament, Tübingen

ZNW   *Zeitschrift für die neutestamentliche Wissenschaft und die Kunde der älteren Kirche*, Giessen, Berlin

ZTK   *Zeitschrift für Theologie und Kirche*, Tübingen

I

ABBA

1. GOD AS 'FATHER' IN THE OLD TESTAMENT

FROM earliest times, the Near East has been familiar with the mythological idea that the deity is the father of mankind or of certain human beings.[1] Peoples, tribes and families picture themselves as being the offspring of a divine ancestor. Particularly, it is the king, as representing his people, who enjoys a special share of the dignity and power of a divine father. Whenever the word 'Father' is used for a deity in this connection it implies fatherhood in the sense of unconditional and irrevocable authority.

All this is a mere commonplace in the history of religion. But it is less well known that from a very early stage the word 'Father' as an epithet for the deity also has another connotation. In a famous Sumerian and Accadian hymn from Ur, the moon god Nanna, or, by his Accadian name, Sin, is invoked as

> Begetter, merciful in his disposing,
> who holds in his hand the life of the whole land.[2]

And it is said of the Sumerian-Babylonian god Ea:

> His wrath is like the deluge,
> his being reconciled like a merciful father.[3]

For orientals, the word 'Father', as applied to God, thus encompasses, from earliest times, something of what the word 'Mother' signifies among us.

Both these aspects of fatherhood, absolute authority and

[1] W. Marchel, *Abba, Père! La prière du Christ et des Chrétiens* (Analecta Biblica 19), Rome 1963, pp. 9-44.
[2] German translation: A. Falkenstein, in: A. Falkenstein – W. von Soden, *Sumerische und akkadische Hymnen und Gebete* (Bibliothek der Alten Welt. Der Alte Orient), Zürich-Stuttgart 1953, p. 223; *ET* by Ferris J. Stephens, in: J. B. Pritchard, *Ancient Near Eastern Texts relating to the Old Testament*[2], Princeton, New Jersey, 1955, p. 385.
[3] von Soden, *op. cit.*, p. 298.

tenderness, are also characteristic of the Old Testament statements about God as 'Father'. God is seldom spoken of as 'Father' in the Old Testament, in fact only fifteen times.[4] By being called 'Father', God is honoured as the Creator:

> Is not he your father, who created you,
> who made you and established you? (Deut. 32.6)

> Have we not all one father?
> Has not one God created us? (Mal. 2.10)[5]

As the Creator, God is the Lord. His will prevails. He can expect to be honoured by obedience.[6] On the other hand, the epithet 'Father' is also used to praise God for his tenderness:

> As a father pities his children,
>   so the Lord pities those who fear him.
> For he knows our frame;
>   he remembers that we are dust. (Ps. 103.13f.)[7]

It is quite obvious that the Old Testament reflects the ancient oriental concept of divine fatherhood. Still, there are fundamental differences. Not the least of them is that in the Old Testament, God the Father and Creator is not thought of as ancestor or progenitor. There is nothing in the Old Testament comparable to an address like

> O father begetter of gods and men;[8]

a passage such as Ps. 2.7 which states that God has 'begotten' an individual, the king, refers to an act of adoption rather than to any physical relationship. It is even more important that in the Old

---

[4] Deut. 32.6; II Sam. 7.14 (par. I Chron. 17.13; 22.10; 28.6); Ps. 68.5; 89.26; Isa. 63.16 (*bis*); 64.8; Jer. 3.4, 19; 31.9; Mal. 1.6; 2.10. (These are only the passages in which God is *called* 'Father', not those in which he is *compared* with an earthly father (e.g. Deut. 1.31; 8.5; Ps. 103.13; Prov. 3.12) or in which Israel is called his son (e.g. Hos. 11.1) or his firstborn (e.g. Ex. 4.22). The actual use of the title 'Father' for God seems to have been more widespread than these examples show, as is suggested by personal names which contain אב as a theophorous element (אֲבִיאֵל ,יוֹאָב, cf. the survey in Marchel,

op. cit., pp. 27f.). Non-Israelite influences may have had some effect here (cf. 'Father' as an address to a foreign god in Jer. 2.27).

[5] Cf. also Isa. 64.8f. (see below, p. 14).

[6] Deut. 14.1; Mal. 1.6 etc. (see below, p. 14).

[7] Cf. also 'father of the fatherless' (Ps. 68.5).

[8] In the hymn to the moon-god cited above (Falkenstein, *op. cit.*, p. 223; Pritchard, *ANET*, p. 385).

Testament, divine fatherhood is related to Israel alone in a quite
unparalleled manner. Israel has a particular relationship to God.
Israel is God's first-born, chosen out of all peoples (Deut. 14.1f.).
Moses is to tell Pharaoh:

> Israel is my first-born son. (Ex. 4.22)

In Jer. 31.9, we find:

> For I am a father to Israel,
> and Ephraim is my first-born.

The decisively new factor here is that the election of Israel as
God's first-born has been made manifest *in a historical action*, the
Exodus from Egypt.[9] Combining God's fatherhood with a
historical action involves a profound revision of the concept of
God as Father. The certainty that God is Father and Israel his son
is grounded not in mythology but in a unique act of salvation by
God, which Israel had experienced in history. Down the centuries,
Israel's sonship on this basis has been felt to be Israel's greatest
privilege. Paul, too, mentions adoption first among God's
gracious gifts to Israel, in Rom. 9.4: $\dot{\omega}\nu$ $\dot{\eta}$ $\upsilon io\theta\epsilon\sigma ia$.

It was not, however, until the *prophets* that the concept of God
as Father gained its full significance in the Old Testament, that the
profundity of the relationship and the seriousness of the demands
contained in it were brought out. Again and again, the prophets
are obliged to say that Israel repays God's fatherly love with
constant ingratitude. Most of the prophetic statements about God
as Father passionately and emphatically point to the obvious
contradiction between Israel's sonship and its godlessness.

> Have you (Israel) not just now called to me,
>   'My father, thou art the friend of my youth—
> will he be angry for ever,
>   and will he be indignant to the end?'
> Behold, you have spoken,
>   but you have done all the evil that you could. (Jer. 3.4f.)

> I thought how I would set you (Israel) among my sons
>   and give you a pleasant land . . .
> And I thought you would call me 'My Father',
>   and would not turn from following me.
> But surely . . . you have been faithless to me, O house of Israel,
>   says the Lord. (Jer. 3.19f.)

[9] Isa. 63.16; Jer. 3.19; Hos. 11.1.

So Israel is put on trial.

> His children have dealt corruptly with him . . .
>> they are a perverse and crooked generation.
> Do you thus requite the Lord,
>> you foolish and senseless people?
> Is not he your father, who created you,
>> who made you and established you? (Deut. 32.5f.)

> Have we not all one father?
>> Has not one God created us?
> Why then are we faithless to one another,
>> profaning the covenant of our fathers? (Mal. 2.10)

> A son honours his father,
>> and a servant his master.
> If then I am a father, where is my honour?
>> and if I am a master, where is my fear? (Mal. 1.6)

Israel's constant answer to this call to repentance is the cry:

Thou art my (or: our) father אַתָּה (וּ) אָבִי

In Third Isaiah, this cry, which is obviously a stereotyped phrase because it occurs several times and in different contexts,[10] is elaborated into a final appeal for God's mercy and forgiveness:

> Look down from heaven and see,
>> from thy holy and glorious habitation.
> Where are thy zeal and thy might?
>> The yearning of thy heart and thy compassion?
> Do not withhold from me,
>> for thou art our Father,
> though Abraham does not know us
>> and Israel does not acknowledge us;
> thou, O Lord, art our Father,
>> 'our Redeemer' from of old is thy name. (Isa. 63.15f.)

> Yet, O Lord, thou art our Father;
>> we are the clay, and thou art our potter;
>> we are all the work of thy hand.
> Be not exceedingly angry, O Lord,
>> and remember not iniquity for ever. (Isa. 64.8f.)

God always answers this appeal of Israel with *forgiveness*. Hos. 11.1-11 draws a touching picture of this. God is compared to a father who taught his little son Ephraim to walk and carried him in his arms:

[10] With אָבִי: Jer. 3.4; Ps. 89.26 (see below, p. 21); cf. Jer. 2.27; with אָבִינוּ: Isa. 63.16 (*bis*); 64.8 (see below, p. 24).

Yet it was I who taught Ephraim to walk,
  I took them up in my arms . . .
How can I give you up, O Ephraim!
  How can I hand you over, O Israel! (Hos. 11.3, 8)

The prophet Jeremiah expresses God's forgiveness in the most moving way. Here God is appealing to his ungrateful people, who have broken faith with him despite all the tokens of his grace:

Return, O faithless sons,
  I will heal your faithlessness. (Jer. 3.22)

With weeping they shall come,
  and with consolations I will lead them back,
I will make them walk by brooks of water,
  in a straight path in which they shall not stumble;
for I am a father to Israel,
  and Ephraim is my first-born. (Jer. 31.9)

God's fatherly mercy exceeds all human comprehension and must prevail:

Is Ephraim my dear son?
  Is he my darling child? . . .
Therefore my heart yearns for him;
  I must have mercy on him, says the Lord. (Jer. 31.20)

This is the Old Testament's final word about the divine father-hood: God's incomprehensible mercy and forgiveness *must* be exercised.

2. GOD AS 'FATHER' IN ANCIENT PALESTINIAN JUDAISM[1]

(i) *The evidence*

Although one still frequently comes across the assertion that 'Father' was a common designation for God in the Judaism of the time of Jesus,[2] there is no evidence for it in the sources—at any rate, those of Palestinian Judaism. On the contrary, there are *amazingly few* instances before the New Testament period. God is described as 'Father' in only four passages in the Apocrypha—that is, those which come from Palestine[3]—and two of these are uncertain and should probably be deleted.[4] Similarly, there are

---

[1] T. W. Manson, *The Teaching of Jesus*², Cambridge 1935 = 1948, pp. 92f.; G. Schrenk, πατήρ *A, C-D, TWNT* V (1954), p. 977. 28ff.; Marchel, *op. cit.*, pp. 83-97.
[2] E.g. S. V. McCasland, 'Abba, Father', *JBL* 72 (1953), p. 84. His whole investigation is based on this erroneous presupposition.
[3] I.e. leaving aside III Macc. 5.7; 6.3, 8; 7.6; Wisdom 2.16; 11.10; 14.3.
[4] Tobit 13.4: 'Because he is our Lord and God, he is our Father for ever.' Sirach 51.10 (Hebrew): 'I praised the Lord: Thou art my Father.' Sirach 23.1, 4 are doubtful (see below, pp. 28f.).

only quite isolated examples in the Pseudepigrapha,[5] and so far
the Qumran literature has produced only one instance: 1QH 9.35.[6]
In Pseudo-Philo, *Liber antiquitatum biblicarum*, God is never
addressed or described as 'Father' and is not even compared with
a father.[7]

There are rather more instances in Rabbinic literature. This
development is evidently connected with the emergence of a new
vocabulary. Johanan b. Zakkai, a contemporary of the apostles,
who taught *c.* AD 50-80, seems to be the first to use the designation
'heavenly Father' ('our heavenly Father', or 'Israel's heavenly
Father') for God; it is associated with him twice.[8] That does not,
of course, mean that Johanan himself coined this phrase; the
extent to which it occurs in the gospel tradition (Mark 11.25;
Matt. 20 times; cf. Luke 11.13, see below, p. 37; Gospel of the
Nazareans, see below, p. 34) suggests the contrary. But Johanan
may well have had a decisive influence in the introduction of the
popular phrase[9] into theological language. It is certainly not a
coincidence that the considerable increase in the use of the

---

[5] Jub. 1.24f., 28 (see below, pp. 20f.); 19.29 (see below, p. 21, n. 37). There
is a suspicion that Test. Levi. 18.6 (φωνὴ πατρική) and Test. Juda 24.2 (ἐκχέαι
πνεῦμα εὐλογίαν πατρὸς ἁγίου) may be Christian.

[6] See below, p. 19.

[7] Report by Pastor Dr C. Dietzfelbinger (Letter of 5 June 1964).

[8] *Mek. Ex.* on 20.25 par. *Siphra Lev.* on 20.16 and *Tos. B.Q.* 7.7 (358.16f.,
here anonymous). The stones of the altar 'create peace between (the) Israel
(ites) and אביהם שבשמים'; *Tos. Ḥag.* 2.1 (234.2-6) par. *j. Ḥag.* 2.77a. 52-54:
'Blessed be the Lord, the God of Israel, who has given our father Abraham
a son (viz. Eleazar b. Arak) who can study and understand the glory of אבינו
שבשמים....'

[9] It might be supposed that the description of God as 'heavenly' father
came from children's language. In itself, such a theory is quite possible, but
there is no evidence for it outside the New Testament. P. Winter, 'Lc 2.49
and Targum Yerushalmi', *ZNW* 45 (1954), pp. 145-79 (and an addendum,
ZNW 46, 1955, pp. 140f.), thought that he could demonstrate that children
had been taught to speak of God as their father before Jesus and his time,
and referred to *Targ. Jerus. II* (Fragment Targum) *Ex.* 15.2, which says that
after the Exodus, infants at the breast made signs to their fathers and called to
them: דֵין הוּא אֲבוּנָן (God), and to Luke 2.49, where the twelve year old
Jesus speaks of remaining ἐν τοῖς τοῦ πατρός μου. But the clause דֵין
הוּא אֲבוּנָן in *Targ. Jerus. II Ex.* 15.2 is hardly as ancient as Winter claims, as the
whole passage about the infants is lacking in Cod. Paris. 110, which M. Ginsburger used as the basis for his edition of the Fragment Targum (Berlin 1899).
Moreover, as Dr B. Schaller reports, *Targ. Neofiti I Ex.* 15.2 does not have it
either in the text or in the marginalia. The passage is thus undoubtedly a
decorative addition.

designation 'heavenly Father' in the tradition of the words of Jesus, as it is reflected in the Gospel of Matthew, comes at the time when Johanan was most active (50-80); the tradition which Matthew took over was moulded in the decades before AD 80.

The new terminology soon found acceptance. It recurs in the great teachers at the end of the first century: Gamaliel II,[10] Eliezer b. Hyrcanus[11] and Eleazar b. Azariah,[12] and throughout the following period.[13] Wherever the Rabbis speak of God as 'Father', they regularly add the complement 'heavenly' (literally, 'who (is) in heaven')[14]; it also finds its way into the *Fragment Targum*[15] and the *Kaddish*.[16]

There can, however, be no question of saying that 'heavenly Father' had become the predominant designation for God. Two things speak against that. First, the relative sparsity of occurrences continues. There are only seven in the *Mishnah*, eleven in the *Tosephta*,[17] four in *Mek. Ex.*,[18] five in *Siphra Lev.*,[19] and none at all in *Gen. Rabbah*.[20] In the *Targum on the Prophets* there is, indeed, a marked reluctance to apply the title 'Father' to God[21]: אָבִי in the Old Testament is twice rendered as רִבּוֹנִי[22] and in other passages

---

[10] Thus at least in the late *Midr. Esth.* 1.1: The cause of the persecution in the days of Ahasuerus (= Xerxes) was that 'the beloved sons angered their heavenly Father' (the name of Gamaliel is missing in the parallel, *Midr. Abba Gorion*, beginning, Billerbeck I, p. 219).

[11] *Soṭah* 9.15: 'On whom can we depend? (Only) on our Father in heaven'; *Midr. Ps.* 25 §13 (ed. Buber, Wilna, 1891, p. 214) on 25.14: 'May it be pleasing before our heavenly Father.'

[12] *Siphra Lev.* on 20.26: 'My Father in heaven so provided for me.'

[13] R. Ishmael (died 135) and his pupils: R. Akiba (died after 135); R. Simeon b. Yohai (*c.* 150); R. Eliezer b. Jose (*c.* 150); R. Nathan (*c.* 160); R. Phineas b. Jair (*c.* 180); R. Simeon b. Eleazar (*c.* 190); R. Judah b. Tema (uncertain, before 200). This list, which is based on the investigations by A. Marmorstein, *The Old Rabbinic Doctrine of God*, I, London 1927, pp. 56-62, 136, should be complete for the Tannaitic period. Notice that a relatively small number of teachers use the phrase 'heavenly Father'; notice, too, that we have only one, or at most two, instances for each of the persons named.

[14] Billerbeck I, p. 393.

[15] *Targ. Jerus. II Ex.* 1.19, 21; 17.11.

[16] The petition for prayers to be heard קדם אבונא דבשמיא is an expansion; cf. I. Elbogen, *Der jüdische Gottesdienst in seiner geschichtlichen Entwicklung*[3], Frankfurt 1931 = [4]Hildesheim 1962, p. 94.

[17] This does not include two passages (*Ta'an.* 3.8 (see below, n. 48) and *Tos. Men.* 7.9 (522.8)) in which God is compared with an earthly father.

[18] Marmorstein, *op. cit.*, pp. 121f. (also a fifth passage, a *varia lectio*).

[19] *Op. cit.*, p. 136, n. 29.   [20] *Op. cit.*, p. 143.

[21] G. Dalman, *The Words of Jesus*, I, *ET*, Edinburgh 1902, p. 191; Marchel, *op. cit.*, pp. 110f.

[22] *Targ. Jer.* 3.4, 19.

אָבִינוּ in the Old Testament is paraphrased metaphorically.[23]

Outside normative Judaism—for example in the *Hebrew* [*III*] *Enoch*—it is quite unheard of for God to be spoken of as Father after the New Testament period. Titles which describe God's power and holiness stand in the foreground. Secondly, a frequent use of this particular title is made unlikely by the fact that when the designation 'heavenly Father' is used, the sense of the words is always remembered, which is not the case with other periphrases of the divine name.[24]

(ii) *The meaning*

With very few exceptions, two convictions, both connected with the message of the prophets, are expressed in any mention of the Fatherhood of God. First to be felt is the *obligation to obey God*, and in practice that means adherence to the Torah. A few representative examples out of many may be cited. Eleazar b. Azariah (*c.* AD 100) taught:

Do not say: 'I have no desire to wear (clothing made of different sorts of stuff), to eat pork, to have intercourse with a woman within the prohibited degrees (because of incest, Lev. 18.6-18)', but (say): 'I do (indeed) desire these things (but) what shall I do, seeing that my heavenly Father has prohibited them?' (*Siphra Lev.* on 20.26)[25]

The obligation to obey the heavenly Father even extends to martyrdom. In an account of Hadrian's persecution by R. Nathan (*c.* 160), we read the following:

Why will you be scourged? . . . These blows are the occasion of my being loved by my heavenly father. (*Mek. Ex.* on 20.6)[26]

Only those who are obedient in this way can be certain of God's Fatherhood. R. Simeon b. Eleazar (*c.* 190) remarks:

[23] *Targ. Isa.* 63.16 (*bis*); 64.7 (see below, p. 20). Cf. also how Jer. 31.9 'For I am a father to Israel' is rendered 'For my *memra* is like a father to Israel' (*Targ. Jer.* 31.9) and Mal. 1.6 'If I am a father' is rendered 'If I am *like* a father' (*Targ. Mal.* 1.6).

[24] G. F. Moore, *Judaism in the First Centuries of the Christian Era*, II, Cambridge 1927, p. 204.

[25] Further instances of the obligation to obey the heavenly Father: *Pirk. Ab.* 5.20 (see below, p. 22); *Kil.* 9.8; *Tos. Kil.* 5.21 (80.26); *Tos. Dem.* 2.9 (47.29-48.1); *Pesik. R.* 27; *Midr. Esth.* 1.1 (see above, p. 17, n. 10) etc.

[26] The parallel passages *Lev. R.* 32 on 24.10 and *Midr. Ps.* 12 §5 (ed. Buber, Wilna 1891, pp. 108f.) on Ps. 12.9 give R. Nehemiah (*c.* 150) as the author.

Anyone who wears clothes of different sorts of stuff 'transgresses and makes his Father in heaven transgress'.[27]

R. Eleazar b. Jose (*c.* 180) says:

All good deeds and works of love which the Israelites have practised in this world are great peace(makers) and great advocates between them and their heavenly Father.[28]

And there is an anonymous saying:

Although all things are the work of my hands, I will reveal myself as father and maker only to him who does my will.[29]

These passages clearly show that fulfilling the Torah brings a man near to God, makes him a child of God, and that disobeying the Torah alienates the child from his father. There are, however, objections to this attitude:

R. Judah (*c.* 150) said:

> If you behave like children,
>   you are called children;
> If you do not behave like children,
>   you are not called children.

But R. Meir (*c.* 150) said:

> Either way—you are called children.[30]

For R. Meir, sin cannot dissolve the relationship in which man is a child of God. But his is just one isolated voice. The dominant thought is that God is the father of the righteous; ideas of merit obscure the idea of the father.

The use of the name 'Father' for God in Palestinian Judaism expresses a second certainty: God is the *one who helps in time of need*; he is the only helper, when no-one else can help. One example of this is the text from the Qumran literature to which reference has already been made, 1QH 9.35f.:

> My father knows me not
> and in comparison with thee my mother has abandoned me.
> But thou art a father to all [the sons] of thy truth
> and as a woman who tenderly loves her babe
> so dost thou rejoice in them:
> and as a foster-father bearing a child in his lap,
> so carest thou for all thy creatures.

[27] *Kil.* 9.8.   [28] *b. B.B.* 10a (Bar.) par. *Tos. Pea* 4.21 (24.31-25.3).
[29] *Ex. R.* 46 on 34.1.
[30] *b. Qid.* 36a (Bar.). Cf. also Moore, *op. cit.*, p. 203, n. 4.

With God the 'true sons'—and, of course, only they—are safe, as
with father and mother. And R. Eliezer b. Hyrcanus (c. 90) ends
his lament at religious decline since the destruction of the Temple
with the question:

> On whom can we depend?
> (Only) on our heavenly Father.[31]

God's goodness is especially expressed in his fatherly forgiveness. R. Meir (c. 150)[32] has the prophet Jeremiah speaking in God's
name to Israel like this:

> My sons, if you return,
> will you not return to your Father?[33]

God's mercy towards Israel is greater than that of an earthly
father:

> Thou art he whose mercy towards us is greater than that of a father
> towards his sons.[34]

This mercy must also be the standard for the conduct of the sons:

> Be merciful on earth,
> as our Father in heaven is merciful.[35]

Here we cannot fail to recognize the nucleus of the message of the
prophets, even if it is embedded in legalistic thought.

On the other hand, there are only quite isolated hints of the
elements of the prophetic message which speak of God as Father
in the future, as in Hosea 1:10 ('It shall be said to them, "Sons of
the living God"') and the prophecy of Nathan in II Sam. 7.14
('I will be his father and he shall be my son'). These are echoed,
for example, in Jub. 1.24: 'I will be their father and they shall be

---

[31] *Soṭah* 9.15.

[32] He has just been mentioned in connection with an analogous statement.

[33] *Deut. R.* 2.24 on 4.30. Further instances: *Yoma* 8.9 ('R. Akiba said,
"Happy are you Israel! Who is it before whom you become clean? And who
is it that makes you clean? Your heavenly father."' See Ezek. 36.25; Jer.
17.13); *Rosh. Hash.* 3.8; *Mek. Ex.* on 15.25; *Ex. R.* 21 on 14.15; 46 on 34.1;
Midr. Esth. on 4.17; *Targ. Jerus. I Ex.* 1.19; *Deut.* 28.32; *Targ. Jerus. II Ex.*
1.19; *Num.* 21.9 etc.

[34] *Targ. Isa.* 63.16, cf. 64.7.

[35] *Targ. Jerus. I Lev.* 22.28, an exact parallel to Luke 6.36, which suggests
that it is an ancient saying (M. Black, *An Aramaic Approach to the Gospels and
Acts*[2], Oxford 1954, p. 138). But *j. Ber.* 5.9c.21 reads 'I' for 'our Father' and
i. Meg. 4.75c.12 has 'we'.

my children'; 25: 'they shall know that these are my children, and that I am their father in uprightness and righteousness, and that I love them'; 28: 'all shall know that I am the God of Israel and the father of all the children of Jacob.' There seem to be no eschatological connotations at all to 'Father' as a divine title in Rabbinic literature.

What new features are there here which are not to be found in the Old Testament? It is perhaps most significant that God is now repeatedly spoken of as the father of the individual Israelite, in other words, that the relationship with God the Father is also understood to be a personal one. In the Old Testament, the relationship is always between God and Israel. The only exception is when from time to time the king is said to have a personal relationship to God, as his father:

> I will be his father (II Sam. 7.14)
>
> He shall cry to me, 'Thou art my Father,
> my God, and the Rock of my salvation.' (Ps. 89.28)[36]

When God is spoken of as Father in Palestinian Judaism, the saying is predominantly understood in a collective sense. God is the father of Israel, his covenant people, and the Israelites are his sons: ἕνα πατέρα ἔχομεν τὸν θεόν say the Jews in John 8.41.[37] But alongside this we now have repeated sayings which relate the individual to God. The first is probably Sirach 51.10, where the person who prays calls אבי אתה[38]; after this it occurs in phrases

[36] Cf. also Ps. 2.7 and the parallels to II Sam. 7.14 (see above, p. 12, n. 4). —Of course, there are two other examples of the appeal to God 'You are my Father' in the Old Testament as well as Ps. 89.27, at Jer. 2.27 and 3.4 (see above, p. 14); but a personification of the people is the subject of both passages, so that the sense is roughly the same as 'Thou art *our* father', Isa. 63.16; 64.8 (see p. 14).

[37] In Jub. 19.29, Abraham blesses his grandson Jacob with the words: 'And may the Lord God be a father to thee and thou the first-born son, and to the people alway.' In Tobit's hymn of praise (Tobit 13.4) we have: αὐτὸς πατὴρ ἡμῶν εἰς πάντας τοὺς αἰῶνας and in Jos., *Antt.* 5.93: ὁ θεός, πατὴρ καὶ δεσπότης τοῦ Ἑβραίων γένους. There is often the significant phrase, '(the) Israel(ites) and their Father in heaven' (see above, p. 16, n. 8); *Mek. Ex.* on 20.25 par. *Tos. B.Q.* 7.6f. (358.13f., 16f.); *Tos. Shab.* 13 [14]. 5 (129.9) par. *b. Shab.* 116a (Bar.); *Tos. Shek.* 1.6 (174.8). The אבונן which *Targ. Jerus.* I *Deut.* 6.4 inserts into the *credo* which is to be prayed each day is also a significant one: 'Hear, Israel, our father, Yahweh our God, Yahweh is one' (ed. M. Ginsburger, Berlin 1903, p. 313.4). See also p. 16, n. 8 (second quotation). Further passages in Schrenk, *op. cit.*, p. 978, n. 206.

[38] See below, p. 23, n. 51.

like 'his heavenly father' or, quite rarely,[39] 'your heavenly
Father'[40] and 'my heavenly Father'.[41] Here are two examples:
R. Judah b. Tema (exact date unknown, but before 200) used to
say:

> Be as bold as a leopard,
> as swift as an eagle,
> as fleeting as a gazelle,
> and as brave as a lion,
> to do the will of your Father in heaven.[42]

R. Nathan (c. 160), or, according to others, R. Nehemiah (same
period) says in an account of the martyrs of Hadrian's persecution
(its conclusion has already been quoted on p. 18):

> Why do you go out to be killed?
>   Because I circumcised sons of Israel.
> Why do you go out to be burnt?
>   Because I read in the Law.
> Why do you go out to be crucified?
>   Because I ate unleavened bread.
> Why will you be scourged?
>   Because I received the festal bunch (at the Feast of Tabernacles)
>   (cf. Zech. 13.6).
> These blows are the occasion of my being loved
>   by my heavenly father.[43]

This personal reference to God as the heavenly Father represented an essential deepening of the relationship with God. Of
course we must not forget that the instances are few ('my heavenly
Father' occurs in only two passages, see above, n. 41)[44] and that
the phrase אבי שבשמים (Hebrew!) did not have the same
familiar sound that 'my heavenly Father' has for us. In the col-

---

[39] *Tos. Ḥull.* 2.24 (503.20f., referring to Eliezer b. Hyrcanus, *c.* 90); *Siphra
Deut.* 48 on 11.22 (said by R. Simeon b. Yoḥai, *c.* 150; acc. to *Yalkuṭ Ha-makiri*
on Prov. 23.13 said by R. Simeon b. Menasya, *c.* 180); *Kil.* 9.8 par. *Tos. Kil.* 5.21
(80.25, R. Simeon b. Eleazar, *c.* 190); *Gen. R.* 71 on 29.32 (R. Jose b. Hanina,
c. 270); anon.: *b. Ber.* 30a; *Targ. Jerus. II Num.* 21.9; *Targ. Esth. II* 1.1 etc.

[40] *Pirk. Ab.* 5.20 (quoted in what follows). In the New Testament, Matthew
alone offers an analogy to this 'thy Father' (6.4, 6, 18). *j. Maʿas.* 3.50c.11
'your heavenly Father' (plural) also properly belongs here (said to two
individual Israelites).

[41] *Mek. Ex.* on 20.6 (par. *Lev. R.* 32 on 24.10; *Midr. Ps.* 12 §5); *Siphra Lev.*
on 20.26 (both passages are quoted here and on p. 18): אבי שבשמים. (For
Seder Eliyyahu Rabbah 28 see below, p. 28, n. 65).

[42] *Pirk. Ab.* 5.20 par. *b. Pes.* 112a (Bar.).

[43] *Mek. Ex.* on 20.6 (see above, p. 18, n. 26).

[44] Marchel, *op. cit.*, p. 90, says quite wrongly: 'ces affirmations sont assez
fréquentes'.

loquial language of Palestine, אֲבִי had entirely given way to אַבָּא, both in Aramaic and in Hebrew.[45] One can see this in the Mishnah: אַבָּא is always used for 'my father', and never אֲבִי[46]; the same is true, with one exception,[47] for the Tosephta. In the title אֲבִי שֶׁבַּשָּׁמַיִם, not only the addition 'who is in heaven' but also the form אֲבִי, which is obsolete, and so has a time-honoured and solemn sound, express the distance which was still felt to exist between God and man even where God was described as 'my Father'. Similarly, there is no trace in Palestine[48] of the tendency, which is noticeable in Hellenistic Judaism,[49] to elaborate the child-father relationship between man and God and to make it a subjective one in an almost sentimental way. When the individual calls God his heavenly Father, it is always because God is the heavenly Father of Israel and because the individual knows that he is a member of the people of God.[50]

Once the divine fatherhood is understood in a personal way, it follows that God can be addressed directly as 'Father' in prayers. There are only mere suggestions of God being addressed as 'Father' in the Old Testament. Of course, the cry אָבִי אַתָּה (Ps. 89.27 as the prerogative of the king; Sirach 51.10, Heb.[51]) and

[45] See below, pp. 58f.

[46] G. Kittel, *Die Religionsgeschichte und das Urchristentum*, Gütersloh 1932, pp. 92ff.

[47] *Tos. Sheb.* 5.6 (452.1), MSS Erfurt and Vienna; the printed editions have אַבָּא here as well.

[48] In Palestine, there are at best hints of a more familiar use of the name 'father'. J. Leipoldt, *Das Gotteserlebnis Jesu im Lichte der vergleichenden Religionsgeschichte*, Leipzig 1927, p. 5, refers to *Test. Levi* 17.2, which says of the priest of the first jubilee (Moses?) that he will speak with God 'as with a father' and to the prayer for rain by Onias the Circle-maker (see p. 61) *Ta'an.* 3.8: 'Master of the world, thy children have turned their faces to me, for that I am like a son of the house before thee.'

[49] Cf. e.g. *Joseph and Aseneth* 12.14f. (ed. P. Batiffol, *Studia Patristica*, Paris 1889-90, p. 56. 19f.): σὺ μόνος εἶ, κύριε, πατὴρ γλυκὺς καὶ ἀγαθὸς καὶ ἐπιεικής. Τίς γὰρ ἕτερος πατὴρ γλυκὺς καὶ ἀγαθὸς ὡς σύ, κύριε; also 12.8 (p. 55.18ff.): Aseneth compares God with a father who takes his small child into his arms whenever it is frightened and holds it to his breast, and prays God to take her in his arms.

[50] The cosmo-genealogical use of the title 'Father' which can be found in Philo, for example, is alien to Palestinian Judaism proper (cf. A. Schlatter, *Die Theologie des Judentums nach dem Bericht des Josefus*, BFCT II 26, Gütersloh 1932, pp. 24f.; Schrenk, *op. cit.*, p. 978).

[51] Sirach 51.10 Heb.: 'And I praised Yahweh (saying), "Thou art my father; thou art the mighty one of my salvation." ' This cry derives from Ps. 89.26 (see p. 21); the Septuagint translation is very strange: ἐπεκαλεσάμην κύριον πατέρα κυρίου μου, and is presumably influenced by Ps. 110.1.

the people's lament אָבִינוּ אַתָּה (Isa. 64.7 and 63.16 (*bis*) with the words in reverse order), or once in the singular אָבִי אַלּוּף נְעֻרַי אָתָּה ('My father, thou art the friend of my youth', Jer. 3.4), come very near to addressing God as 'Father', but in every case we have a statement, and not a vocative.[52] True, there is a vocative in the divine reproach in Jer. 3.19: 'And I thought you would call me, My Father, and would not turn from following me', but we should not fail to notice that the saying does not blame Israel for failing to call God Father but, as the parallel clause and the context show, for denying that it is a child. The fact that one looks in vain for God to be addressed as Father anywhere in the Psalter or in any other prayer in the Old Testament shows how careful we must be in arguing from any of the passages which have been cited.[53] David's hymn of praise in I Chron. 29.10: בָּרוּךְ אַתָּה יְהוָה אֱלֹהֵי יִשְׂרָאֵל אָבִינוּ מֵעוֹלָם וְעַד־עוֹלָם does not belong here at all. For we should not follow the LXX in translating it:

> Blessed be thou, Yahweh, God of Israel, our father,
> from eternity to eternity,

but translate it:

> Blessed be thou, Yahweh, God of our ancestor Israel,[54]
> from eternity to eternity.

We first meet the title 'Father' as a direct address in prayer in ancient Judaism; but there are only isolated instances in Palestine. In the Diaspora there are rather more. By and large other titles for God are far more frequent in Jewish prayers. From the first two centuries AD we can mention with certainty *only two prayers* from Palestine which address God as Father. The oldest example is likely to be the prayer אהבה רבה (the second of the two benedictions which introduced the morning *Shemaʻ*), which had probably

[52] It is not clear whether אָבִי is a statement or a vocative in Jer. 3.4. Comparisons with Isa. 63.16; 64.7 on the one hand, and Jer. 2.27 on the other, suggest that it is a statement. So too LXX.

[53] This restraint may possibly be connected with the fact that the cry אָבִי אַתָּה had undesirable overtones, as Jer. 2.27 shows: '. . . who say to a tree אָבִי אַתָּה and to a stone, "You gave me birth" ', cf. G. Quell, πατήρ B, *TWNT* V (1954), p. 967.

[54] Cf. *Joseph and Aseneth* 8.9 (p. 49.18f. Batiffol): κύριε ὁ θεὸς τοῦ πατρός μου Ἰσραήλ.

been part of the ancient priests' liturgy, used in temple worship, before that[55]; it runs:

> Our Father, our King (אבינו מלכנו),
> for the sake of our fathers,
> who trusted upon thee
> and whom thou taughtest the statutes of life—
> have mercy upon us and teach us.[56]

The *Litany for the New Year* uses the same address; with an impressive monotony, all its verses begin אבינו מלכנו. Although this Litany was later extended in many places, we can see the extreme age of its basic material, as R. Akiba (died after AD 135) quotes its beginning and its end during a drought:

> Our Father, our king,
>   we have no other king but thee;
> our father, our king,
>   for thine own sake have mercy upon us.[57]

---

[55] The facts about the use of אהבה רבה in the Temple are very complicated. The question is what is meant by the 'praise' (no further details are given) which the priests spoke at the daily morning service in the Temple before the recitation of the Decalogue and the *Shema* according to *Tam.* 5.1. Mar Samuel (died 254) says in *b. Ber.* 11b that this praise was the אהבה רבה; but in *j. Ber.* 1. 3c.24, 34 the tradition is that Samuel taught that it was the 'Torah benediction'. This could refer to the so-called '*Benediction over the Torah*' (text in Billerbeck I, p. 397), but probably refers to אהבה רבה as characterized by its content (I. Elbogen, *Studien zur Geschichte des jüdischen Gottesdienstes*, Berlin 1907, pp. 17f., 25 ; *id. Der jüdische Gottesdienst in seiner geschichtlichen Entwicklung*³, Frankfurt 1931 = ⁴Hildesheim 1962, p. 25 ; Billerbeck IV, p. 192, n. 1). Samuel's contemporary R. Simeon b. Lakish puts forward a different view about the 'praise' of *Tam.* 5.1; his opinion is that it refers to the prayer יוצר אור (*b. Ber.* 11b). The texts are collected in Billerbeck I, pp. 397f. The Babylonian Talmud opts for אהבה רבה at *b. Ber.* 11b, and most modern scholars accept this (Elbogen, *Der jüdische Gottesdienst, ibid.*; Billerbeck IV, p. 192, n. 1; T. W. Manson, *The Teaching of Jesus*², Cambridge 1935 = 1948, p. 92).

[56] *Siddur Sephath Emeth*, ed. W. B. Heidenheim, Rödelheim 1886 (cited from now on as Heidenheim), p. 17a.13f. According to L. Zunz, *Die gottesdienstlichen Vorträge der Juden*², Frankfurt-M. 1892, pp. 382f., the words which come immediately afterwards: 'Our Father, merciful Father, have mercy upon us . . .' (p. 17a.14f.) are a later addition.

[57] *b. Ta'an.* 25b. In view of all that we know about the regularity of liturgical usage, it is erroneous to conclude that the litany developed out of R. Akiba's prayer (so P. Fiebig, *Rosch ha-schana*, Giessen 1914, p. 62; Elbogen, *Der jüdische Gottesdienst*, pp. 147, 276). On the contrary, R. Akiba is quoting the beginning and end of a litany which is already in use (thus K. G. Kuhn, *Achtzehngebet und Vaterunser und der Reim*, WUNT 1, Tübingen 1950, p. 9). H. Kosmala, *Hebräer—Essener—Christen* (Studia post-biblica 1), Leiden 1959, p. 191, n. 3, also rightly concludes that the prayer 'in its simplest form goes back at least to the first century AD, and may be even older'.

It is clear that both instances are liturgical passages; it is the
community which calls upon God as 'our Father'. Moreover, in
both instances אבינו is connected with מלכנו: the father to
whom the community prays is thus the heavenly king.

God is often addressed as אבינו מלכנו again at a later date, in
particular in the 'prayers of imploration' (*Taḥanunim*) with which daily
morning prayer ends, passages which come from different times and
which have been altered in different ways, but which even in their oldest
form can hardly be as old as the two examples which have been quoted.[58]
Otherwise, there is a simple אבינו in several petitions of the *Eighteen
Benedictions*; this, however, is always an addition,[59] as is the אלהינו
אבינו in the third benediction of the grace after meals.[60]

But the two prayers which have just been quoted are by no
means the only evidence for the antiquity of the use of the
address 'Father' to God in prayer. In investigating a form of
address used in prayer we must not limit ourselves to dating the
prayers in which it occurs; we must also take into consideration
the fact that forms of address in prayer stand in a liturgical tradition and can therefore be older than the particular prayer in which
they appear. This could also be true of the address אבינו שבשמים.
True, it appears only in a few Jewish prayers of quite a late date,[61]
but the address in the Matthaean version of the Lord's Prayer
(6.9: πάτερ ἡμῶν ὁ ἐν τοῖς οὐρανοῖς) shows that it was used as early
as the first century AD. On the other hand, the address אב

---

[58] Heidenheim, pp. 23bff.; on this question see Elbogen, *Der jüdische
Gottesdienst*, pp. 73-81.

[59] Marchel, *op. cit.*, p. 86, has not noticed this. The address אבינו occurs
(a) in the fourth benediction (Pal.), but not in the Babylonian recension,
(b) in the fifth benediction (Bab.), but not in the Palestinian recension, (c) in
the sixth benediction (Pal. and Bab.), but here the way in which it spoils the
rhyme shows that it is an addition. Furthermore, the address אבינו does not
appear in any of the three cases in the Eighteen Benedictions as quoted in
j. Ber. 4d.52ff. (though there, of course, they are in an abbreviated form).
Thus the address is an addition in all three benedictions (Kuhn, *op. cit.*,
pp. 13-5). In the *Siddur* according to the German rite, the address has also
found its way into the nineteenth benediction (Bab.), cf. G. Dalman, *Die
Worte Jesu*, I¹, Leipzig 1898, appendix 'Messianic texts', p. 304, n. 3.

[60] L. Finkelstein, 'The Birkat Ha-Mazon', *JQR* 19 (1928-9), pp. 211-62;
J. Jeremias, *The Eucharistic Words of Jesus*, ET², London 1966, p. 110, n. 12.

[61] E.g. in the late (Elbogen, *op. cit.*, p. 92) section אתה הוא from the
morning prayers (Heidenheim, p. 3b.2f.); in a late introduction to the Hymn
of Moses (G. Dalman, *Die Worte Jesu*, I², Leipzig 1930, p. 296, Aramaic);
several times in the still later (see below, p. 28) *Seder Eliyyahu Rabbah* (ed.
Friedmann, Vienna 1902), ch. 7 (p. 33.2); ch. 18 (*ter*) (pp. 112.18, 21; 115.6);
also in the Warsaw edition, 1883: ch. 21 (p. 188.5).

הרחמיב,[62] which a similar argument (cf. II Cor. 1.3) proves to be
an ancient one,[63] does not belong here; in this case God is not
addressed as 'Father', with the genitive characterizing the
Father' as being merciful, but 'Father' is a specifying word, by
which a property is attributed to someone as his dominant
characteristic: 'Thou embodiment of mercy.'

The two earliest instances of God being addressed as 'Father'
ran, 'Our Father, our King'. It is most important to discover
whether *God is also addressed as 'my Father'* in early Palestinian
Judaism. It is certain that God was addressed as πάτερ in Diaspora
Judaism,[64] which followed the example of the Greek world here.

---

[62] The address אב הרחמים occurs twice in the liturgy which frames the
reading of the Torah, which is still unknown to Talmudic sources (Elbogen,
op. cit., p. 198), namely in the two prayers which begin similarly אב הרחמים
(Heidenheim, p. 27a.3 = 53b.28 and p. 55a.14); in fact, the second of these
prayers was only introduced after the Crusades (Elbogen, *op. cit.*, p. 203); it
also occurs in the passage מי כמוך which has been inserted into the second
petition of the *Eighteen Benedictions* (Heidenheim, p. 19b.5) and is first attested
in the ninth century (Elbogen, *op. cit.*, p. 45); finally, it is used twice in the
Habhdala at the end of the Sabbath in the prayer רבון העולמים (Heidenheim,
p. 90b.2, 17), of uncertain date (hardly identical with the prayer רבון
העולמים mentioned by R. Johanan (died 279) in *b. Yoma* 87b, which was appointed for the eve of the Day of Atonement. Prayers beginning רבון כל העולמים
or רבון של עולם occur repeatedly, cf. Elbogen, *op. cit.*, Index, [2]p. 617 = [4]p.
633). There are a number of other occasions in the same prayer רבון
העולמים in which God is addressed as האב הרחמן (Heidenheim, p. 90b.9), but
these are later additions. They are also to be found in the prayer אהבה רבה
mentioned above, in the prayer ברוך שאמר (Heidenheim, p. 7b.26; Elbogen,
op. cit., pp. 83f.) which is first mentioned in the ninth century, and in the
prayer הטה (Heidenheim, p. 24a.1), which belongs to the *Taḥanunim* (see
above, p. 26), which is also of uncertain date.

[63] Of course the phrase ὁ πατὴρ τῶν οἰκτιρμῶν in II Cor. 1.3, a Semitism
which is not attested elsewhere outside the prayers mentioned in n. 62, is not
used as an address in prayer by Paul, but is part of a eulogy with stereotyped
formulas. This suggests that it was not composed by the apostle for the
occasion, but was already to hand.

[64] III Macc. 6.3, 8; *Apocryphon Ezek.* frag. 3 (quoted I Clem. 8.3, without
mentioning the source, and in Clem. Alex., *Paed.* I, 91.2 [I, p. 143.20 Stählin]);
Wisdom 14.3. The inscription on a Jewish tomb, J.-B. Frey, *Corpus In-
scriptionum Iudaicarum* (Sussidi allo studio delle antichità cristiane 1), Rome
1936, pp. 135f., no. 193 (Rome, undated): [. . . νο]μομαθὴς [. . .] ἀμίαντος
[ἔζησεν ἔτη . . .] ἡμέρας ιβ΄ [. . .]αε μίμησω (= μέμνησο) πάτερ [μετὰ
πάντω ?]ν τῶν δικαίων does not belong here. There is no analogy to the use
of πάτερ as an address to God on an inscription (in any case, direct addresses
are rare). Presumably the dead person is being addressed here (Frey, *op. cit.*, p.
cxxxvii). God is not addressed as πάτερ in Josephus (A. Schlatter, *Die
Theologie des Judentums nach dem Bericht des Josefus*, BFCT II 26, Gütersloh 1932,
p. 24) or in Philo.

In Palestine, however, we have only one double example, in
Sirach 23.1, 4 (beginning of the second century BC):

$$\kappa\acute{\upsilon}\rho\iota\epsilon\ \pi\acute{a}\tau\epsilon\rho\ \kappa a\grave{\iota}\ \delta\acute{\epsilon}\sigma\pi o\tau a\ \zeta\omega\hat{\eta}s\ \mu o\upsilon$$
$$\kappa\acute{\upsilon}\rho\iota\epsilon\ \pi\acute{a}\tau\epsilon\rho\ \kappa a\grave{\iota}\ \theta\epsilon\grave{\epsilon}\ \zeta\omega\hat{\eta}s\ \mu o\upsilon$$

(the *Seder Eliyyahu Rabbah*, in which God is frequently addressed
in the singular as 'my Father in heaven', Hebrew אבי שבשמים,[65]
is excluded because of the late date of its composition [*c.* AD 974],[66]
and the place of its origin [Southern Italy]). Here, and only here,
God is addressed by a writer from ancient Palestinian Judaism as
'my Father', and we would have to commend this passage as a
prologue to the Gospel[67]—were not the wording given by the
LXX extremely doubtful. Sirach 23 is one of the parts of the book
of Sirach for which we do not have the original Hebrew text.
We do, however, possess a prosodic Hebrew paraphrase (of
course, a late one) of the passage (MS Adler 3053). In this, *κύριε
πάτερ* is represented by אל אבי,[68] but that means 'God of my
father', and not 'God, my Father'! Now as the address 'God of my
father' appears in Sirach and, indeed, in the form אלהי אבי in the
extant Hebrew text of ch. 51 (v. 1),[69] and also elsewhere,[70] we are

---

[65] The address אבי שבשמים occurs in ch. 10 (ed. Friedmann, p. 51.10);
ch. 17 (p. 83.24); ch. 18 (p. 100.10); in ch. 19 six times according to Friedmann's edition (p. 110.10; 111.27; 112.3, 6, 9, 14) and ten times according to
the Warsaw edition, 1883; ch. 20 (ed. Friedmann, p. 121.20) and ch. 28
(p. 149.9). In the last-mentioned passage the address 'my Father in heaven' is
even anachronistically put in the mouth of R. Zadok (50-80). The quite
singular and frequent appearance of the address in the mediaeval Midrash
can only be explained as a peculiarity of its author. As he lived in Southern
Italy, Christian influence may well be possible. Note that the address is אבי
and not אבא.

[66] Zunz, *op. cit.*, p. 119. J. Mann, 'Changes in the Divine Service of the
Synagogue due to Religious Persecutions', *HUCA* 4 (1927), pp. 241-310,
here pp. 302-10 ('Appendix. Date and Place of Redaction of Seder Eliyahu
Rabba and Zuṭṭa'), has argued for a rather earlier date (second half of the
fifth century). I. Ziegler, 'Tanna děbe Elijahu', *Jüdisches Lexikon* V (1930),
cols. 864f., simply reports both views, but seems to suggest that he agrees
with Zunz (with editorial assent from I. Elbogen).

[67] This phrase comes, I think, from P. Batiffol.

[68] J. Marcus, 'A Fifth MS of Ben Sira', *JQR* 21 (1930-1), p. 238.

[69] The parallelism confirms that there is a construct, and not a vocative
('God, my father') in Sirach 51.1: 'I will give thanks to thee, O God of my
salvation (cf. Ps. 18.46 אֱלֹהֵי יִשְׁעִי), I will praise thee, O God of my father
(cf. Ex. 15.2 אֱלֹהֵי אָבִי).

forced to conclude that the Hebrew text of Sirach 23.1, 4 had the phrase 'God of my father', which comes from Exod. 15.2, and not 'Lord, my Father'.[71] In short, although the community prays to God as Father in the words אבינו מלכנו, although the individual occasionally speaks of God as his heavenly Father: אבי שבשמים, *there is as yet no evidence in the literature of ancient Palestinian Judaism that 'my Father' is used as a personal address to God.*

[70] 'God of my father' in the vocative: Gen. 32.9 (*bis*); Esther 4.17m A; Judith 9.2, 12; cf. (not in the vocative): Gen. 31.5, 42; Ex. 15.2; 18.4. The plural form of the address is more frequent: 'God of my fathers' (Dan. 2.23; I Esdr. 8.25 *v.l.*; *j. Ber.* 4.7d.29, 32), 'God of our fathers' (I Chron. 29.10, 18; II Chron. 20.6; Dan. 3.26, 52; Tobit 8.5; *Pirḳ. Ab.* 5.20c) or simply 'God of the fathers' (Wisdom 9.1; I Esdr. 4.60). Very frequent outside the vocative, e.g. Acts 5.30; 22.14. (It is difficult to decide between nominative and vocative in 1QM 13.7: 'But [thou] (art?) God of our fathers'.)

[71] Note that according to the translation rules of the translator of Sirach it is extremely probable that the κύριε πάτερ of the Septuagint (Sirach 23.1, 4) represents a אלהי אבי, as LXX Sirach on an overwhelming number of occasions renders אלהים with κύριος (nineteen times, and only four times with θεός). The Septuagint understood אלהי אבי as a double vocative instead of as a single vocative composed of a noun in the construct and a genitive. The same mistake crept in at Sirach 51.1, where it translates אלהי אבי as κύριε βασιλεῦ and not as κύριε τοῦ πατρός μου (see above, n. 69).

3. JESUS

A. 'Father' as a title for God in the sayings of Jesus

(i) The tradition

No less than one hundred and seventy times in the gospels, we find the word 'Father' for God on the lips of Jesus. At first glance there does not appear to be the least doubt that for Jesus 'Father' was *the* designation for God. But is this really true? When we tabulate the number of instances in which the name 'Father' is used by Jesus in the gospels, we find that the result is startling. The occurrences are distributed as follows:

Mark	4	Matthew[1]	42
Luke[1]	15	John	109

How are we to explain this extremely striking difference in the figures?

[1] In Matt. 11.27 par. Luke 10.22 in which πατήρ occurs three times, only the first πατήρ is counted, for reasons which will be given later (see below, pp. 47f.). This should also be remembered in the other figures which follow.

The problem becomes even more acute if, first, we exclude the passages in which God is addressed as 'Father' in prayers, which require separate treatment (see pp. 54ff.; in that case we lose one example from Mark, six from Luke, five from Matthew and nine from John, see the table on p. 54) and secondly, if we subdivide the table so that parallel texts appear only *once* (thus in the following table the instances in which Matthew and Luke have taken over the title 'Father' from Mark are only counted under Mark, and the instances common to Matthew and Luke are listed as a separate group). The result is the following enumeration of instances of the use of the title 'Father' for God in the words of Jesus:

Mark	3^2
Common to Matthew and Luke	4^3
Additional instances peculiar to Luke	4^4
Additional instances peculiar to Matthew	31^5
John	100

This table shows that *there was a growing tendency to introduce the title 'Father' for God into the sayings of Jesus.* Mark, the sayings tradition and the special Lucan material all agree in reporting that Jesus used the word 'Father' for God only in a few instances. Only in Matthew is there a noticeable increase, and in John 'the Father' has almost become a synonym for God.[6]

As the number of instances begins to increase with *Matthew*, the question is whether the evangelist himself is responsible for them or whether the process had already begun in the tradition at his disposal. In fact, both alternatives apply.

All in all, Matthew has the name 'Father' forty-two times on the lips of Jesus, and five of these times it is used as an address to God. Of the remaining thirty-seven instances, he has taken over two from Mark[7] and has a further four in common with Luke.[8] Thus thirty-one instances peculiar to Matthew remain. Some of these additional examples

---

[2] Mark 8.38 (par. Matt. 16.27; Luke 9.26); 11.25; 13.32 (par. Matt. 24.36).

[3] Matt. 5.48 (par. Luke 6.36); 6.32 (par. Luke 12.30); 7.11 (par. Luke 11.13); 11.27 (par. Luke 10.22). For the last passage see n. 1.

[4] Luke 2.49; 12.32; 22.29; 24.49.

[5] Matt. 5.16, 45; 6.1, 4, 6a, 6b, 8, 14, 15, 18a, 18b, 26; 7.21; 10.20, 29, 32, 33; 12.50; 13.43; 15.13; 16.17; 18.10, 14, 19, 35; 20.23; 23.9; 25.34; 26.29, 53; 28.19.

[6] Incidentally, this development shows the inappropriateness of regarding Mark as an excerpt from Matthew.

[7] Matt. 16.27; 24.36.   [8] See above, n. 3.

certainly derive from Matthew himself: he has inserted πατήρ into the Marcan material four times,[9] and the interpretation of the parable of the tares, which was in all probability written by Matthew himself,[10] ends with τοῦ πατρὸς αὐτῶν. (Matt. 13.43). But the very restraint which Matthew imposes upon himself in inserting πατήρ into the Marcan material (only four instances!) makes it highly unlikely that all thirty-one special Matthaean instances derive from Matthew himself. Time and again, in fact, it can be demonstrated that the key-word 'Father' was already provided for him by the tradition: that this was so in Matt. 6.14f.; 18.35 can be seen from a comparison with Mark 11.25, and in Matt. 10.32f. from a comparison with Mark 8.38.

We can confirm this conclusion by confining our attention for a moment to the phrase 'heavenly Father'. Matthew is distinctive not only in the frequency with which he designates God as 'Father' in general, but also, more particularly, in the frequency of his use of the phrase 'heavenly Father'. It occurs no less than twenty times[11] in his work as compared with once elsewhere in the New Testament, at Mark 11.25 (cf. also Luke 11.13 ὁ πατὴρ ὁ ἐξ οὐρανοῦ). This ratio alone might lead one to suppose that in every single Matthaean passage the phrase 'heavenly Father' should be attributed to the evangelist. The following observations, however, all agree in indicating that such a conclusion would be a false one: (*a*) Mark (11.25) and the pre-Lucan tradition (Luke 11.13, see below, p. 37) know the phrase, so it is not newly created by Matthew. (*b*) While Matthew has indeed inserted the word 'Father' at four points in the Marcan text (see this page, n. 9), 'my heavenly Father' occurs in only one of them (Matt. 12.50); the others merely have 'my Father' (Matt. 20.23; 26.29, 42). Even the interpretation of the parable of the tares (13.36-43), which bears such strong traces of Matthaean linguistic peculiarities that, as has been said above, it may be attributed to Matthew himself, simply has τοῦ πατρὸς αὐτῶν, without any addition, in 13.43. (*c*) Furthermore, there is the variety of formulations:

ὁ πατὴρ (μου, ἡμῶν, ὑμῶν) ὁ ἐν τοῖς οὐρανοῖς eight times[12]
ὁ πατὴρ (μου,   ὑμῶν) ὁ ἐν   οὐρανοῖς five times[13]
ὁ πατὴρ (μου,   ὑμῶν) ὁ   οὐράνιος seven times[14]

[9] Matt. 12.50; 26.29 (for ὁ θεός Mark 3.35; 14.25); 20.23 (addition); further, there is one use of the address πάτερ μου in a prayer (26.42, in a repetition of the prayer Mark 14.36 par. Matt. 26.39).

[10] J. Jeremias, *The Parables of Jesus*, ET², London 1963, pp. 81-5.

[11] 'My heavenly Father' nine times: 7.21; 10.32f.; 12.50; 15.13; 16.17; 18.10, 19, 35; 'Your heavenly Father' ten times: 5.16, 45, 48; 6.1, 14, 26, 32; 7.11; 18.14 (on the variant reading μου see below, p. 38, n. 49); 23.9; once in a prayer 'Our heavenly Father': Matt. 6.9.

[12] Matt. 5.16; 6.1, 9; 7.11, 21; 10.32, 33; 16.17.

[13] Matt. 5.45; 12.50; 18.10, 14, 19.

[14] Matt. 5.48; 6.14, 26, 32; 15.13; 18.35; 23.9.

which makes mock of any attempt at discovering a regular pattern; as a result, it seems likely that these are variant traditions which ante-date Matthew. (*d*) Finally, one ought to draw attention to the address πάτερ ἡμῶν ὁ ἐν τοῖς οὐρανοῖς in the Lord's Prayer, which is an elaboration of the short form πάτερ (Luke 11.2). As it is hardly conceivable that Matthew should have ventured to alter the Lord's Prayer on his own authority, we have a hint of traditional liturgical material in the expanded address. The occurrence of a similar expanded address, though with the singular ἐν τῷ οὐρανῷ, in the Didache (8.2), may serve as confirmation.

All this shows that when the Matthaean sayings speak of God as 'Father' withthe addition of the epithet 'heavenly', the evangelist himself was at work only in individual instances (as in Matt. 12.50). In most cases he found the phrase 'heavenly Father' already before him in the tradition. Thus our earlier (see above, p. 30) conclusion has been confirmed: the *considerable increase in the use of the title 'Father' for God* in the tradition of the words of Jesus *had already begun in the stratum which was available to Matthew.*

So strong is the tendency of the tradition to introduce the word πατήρ into the sayings of Jesus (compare again the table on p. 30 above), that it seems in principle far more probable that we should assume secondary elaboration in all thirty-one instances in which Matthew is the only witness for the word 'Father'. This is particularly true of the eight sayings common to Matthew and Luke in which Matthew has the word 'Father' but Luke does not.[15] That does not, however, exclude the possibility that ancient 'Father' sayings may be concealed in the special Matthaean material, though on analogy with the other synoptic strata there will only be very few of them. The sayings most likely to fall into this category are Matt. 6.14f.; 18.35 (cf. Mark 11.25) and 10.32f. (cf. Mark 8.38).

The New Testament development comes to its logical conclusion in *John*: in the Gospel of John, 'the Father' is the predominant title for God on the lips of Jesus (100 instances, including 9 as an address in prayers). There are two characteristic features of the Fourth Gospel in addition to the peculiar frequency with which the title occurs. First, whereas 'my Father' occurs frequently on the lips of Jesus (25 instances), 'your Father'

[15] Matt. 5.45 (par. Luke 6.35); 6.26 (par. Luke 12.24), on which see below, p. 40; 7.21 (par. Luke 6.46), on which see p. 44; 10.20 (par. Luke 12.12), 29 (par. Luke 12.6), 32f. (par. Luke 12.8f.), on which see pp. 44f.; 18.14 (par. Luke 15.7), on which see p. 39.

fades right into the background (only 20.17, to the disciples, and 8.42, to the Jews). It is important to have noted the tendency of the later tradition to suppress 'your Father' almost to vanishing point when one is assessing the instances when 'my Father' and 'your Father' alternate in parallel sayings in the synoptic tradition. Here 'your Father' consequently has the greater claim to priority (thus Mark 11.25 / Matt. 6.14f. over against Matt. 18.35; Matt. 18.14 אמכ ὑμῶν over against BΘφ μου). Secondly, ὁ πατήρ, used absolutely by Jesus (73 instances), dominates the Gospel of John; before John, there are only quite isolated examples in the Gospels (Mark 13.32 par. Matt. 24.36; Matt. 28.19; Luke 9.26[16]), but it occurs fifteen times in the Johannine epistles and is a favourite designation for God subsequently in the Apostolic Fathers. It is clear that the Johannine writings led to ὁ πατήρ, in the absolute, becoming *the* name of God in Christendom.[17]

The evidence in the *Gospel of Thomas* corresponds to the picture that we find in the Gospel of John, even down to individual details. Here, too, the title 'Father' is the most prominent (20 instances in the 114 logia); indeed, if we exclude two logia which derive from the synoptic tradition[18] and one occurrence of 'the Living One',[19] it is the only title for God. 'My Father' also stands out in the Gospel of Thomas (4 examples),[20] while 'your Father' fades into the background (2 examples)[21]; 'the Father', used absolutely, holds pride of place (12 examples).[22]

How did the title 'Father' for God come to dominate the scene in this way? We can mention some factors which contributed to this development (though they were certainly not the only ones). The first suggests itself if we trace the origin of the phrase 'heavenly Father'. It is a *semitism*, as is shown by the regular use of the plural οἱ οὐρανοί (Mark 11.25; always in Matthew; the singular ὁ πατὴρ ὁ ἐξ οὐρανοῦ occurs once, at Luke 11.13). Now we have already seen that the first evidence of God being called 'heavenly Father' in Palestinian Judaism comes from the first century (with

[16] For Matt. 11.27 par. Luke 10.22, see above, p. 29, n. 1.
[17] T. W. Manson, *The Teaching of Jesus*[2], Cambridge 1935 = 1948, pp. 99f.
[18] 'God' occurs twice in Logion 100, cf. Mark 12.17 par., and 'the Lord' in Logion 73, cf. Matt. 9.38.
[19] In Logion 37, Jesus is called 'the Son of the Living One'. In Logion 59, however, 'the Living One' probably refers to Jesus.
[20] Logia 61, 64, 99 (*bis*).
[21] Logia 15, 50.
[22] Logia 27, 40, 44, 57, 69a, 76, 79, 83, 96, 97, 98, 113. 'The living Father' also occurs twice (3, 50).

Johanan b. Zakkai (*c.* 50-80)[23]) and that it quickly established
itself. As the tradition used by Matthew was shaped over the same
period, it follows that Palestinian Christianity also shared in this
process within Judaism. In Gentile Christian areas, however, the
phrase 'heavenly Father' made no headway; it is not to be found
in the Gospel of John or the Gospel of Thomas, though it survived
in Jewish Christianity.[24]

A second factor operating within Christianity can be seen from
the distribution of the title 'Father' in the Gospel of Matthew: the
thirty-one instances peculiar to the First Gospel are concentrated
in speeches (the passage about the piety of the Pharisees in 6.1-18
(9 instances), the prophecy of persecution in the address when the
twelve are sent out in 10.17-39 (4 instances) and the address about
the duties of the leaders of the community in 18.10-35 (4 instances)),
in eschatological sayings[25] and in instructions.[26] In other words,
the increasing occurrence of the title 'Father' in the sayings of
Jesus is evidently connected with its use in catechesis. The
phenomenon betrays a concern to make the message of Jesus the
personal possession of the faithful. But the starting point for this
catechetical extension of the use of the title 'Father' for God is to
be seen in *prayer*, and above all in the Lord's Prayer. Pauline
linguistic usage points to this. In the Pauline corpus of letters, the
title 'Father' for God occurs almost without exception in liturgical
phrases and in prayers: in the introductions of the letters, particularly in the benedictions of the *salutatio*, in prayers of thanksgiving and intercession, in doxologies, in credal formulas, in texts
with a hymnic ring, and in the spirit-inspired cry 'Abba'. The *lex
orandi* thus determined the *lex credendi*.[27]

Thirdly, and finally, the strong increase in the occurrence of the
title 'Father' which is reflected in the Gospel of John and the
Gospel of Thomas involves a factor which can be traced in
Rev. 2.27; 3.5, 21. Here the exalted Christ speaks of God as 'my
Father'. In other words, *Christian prophets*, who spoke in the name

---

[23] See above, p. 16.
[24] *Gospel of the Hebrews* 7b, 26 (E. Klostermann, *Apocrypha*, II[3], Kleine
Texte 8, Berlin 1929, pp. 7, 12). P. Vielhauer rightly assigns both logia to the
Gospel of the Nazaraeans (in: E. Hennecke – W. Schneemelcher – R. McL.
Wilson, *New Testament Apocrypha*, I, *ET*, London 1963, pp. 147, 150).
[25] Matt. 7.21; 13.43; 15.13; 20.23; 25.34; 26.29.
[26] Matt. 5.16, 45; 23.9, cf. 12.50.
[27] This statement will be confirmed below, p. 36.

of the exalted Lord and with his words, contributed to the increase in the use of the title 'Father' for God in the tradition of the words of Jesus.

In view of the demonstrable tendency of the tradition to introduce the name 'Father' for God into the sayings of Jesus to an ever increasing extent, it might appear doubtful whether Jesus ever used it at all. But we shall see that such scepticism does not do justice to the facts when we discuss the way in which God is addressed as 'Father' in the prayers of Jesus.[28]

(ii) The significance of the title 'Father' for God in the sayings of Jesus

The sparsity of the instances in which God is called 'Father' in Mark (3), in the Matthew-Luke sayings material (4) and in the Lucan special material (4) (see the table on p. 30 above) showed us that we must look for the oldest tradition of our theme in the area of these three synoptic strata. Evidently the material available to the second and third evangelists had already found its way into a Hellenistic milieu and had been stabilized there at the time when the process of the increase of the occurrence of the title 'Father' for God in the sayings of Jesus, reflected in the first Gospel, and more strongly in the Fourth, began in the Jewish Christian area.

That being so, it is advisable for us to begin our investigation with the instances of the title 'Father' which occur in Mark, in the Matthew-Luke sayings material, and in the special Lucan material. We are concerned with 11 passages, which are listed above on p. 30, notes 2-4.[29] First, however, we must make two qualifications. On the one hand, one or two old sayings may be concealed among the 31 instances peculiar to Matthew and the 100 peculiar to John. Of course, they are only recognizable in isolated instances,[30] and their number will not be proportionally much greater than the number of instances in the three synoptic strata from which we begin. On the other hand, the 11 instances from

---

[28] See below, pp. 54ff.

[29] The present work thus makes a much more radical investigation than, say, G. Schrenk in his article πατήρ *A,C-D*, *TWNT* V (1954), pp. 946-59, 974-1016, with which it has a number of points of contact in the exegesis.

[30] See above, p. 30: for example, Mark 11.25 shows that the word 'Father' in Matt. 6.14f. is pre-Matthaean, and Matt. 11.27 par. Luke 10.22 shows that the word 'Father' in John 10.15a is pre-Johannine.

which we begin cannot be regarded as authentic sayings of Jesus without a critical examination.

The 11 instances fall into three groups:

(*a*) Sayings which designate God as ὁ πατήρ without a personal pronoun;

(*b*) Sayings which speak of God as 'your Father';

(*c*) Sayings in which Jesus calls God 'my Father'. The phrase 'the Father of the Son of Man' (Mark 8.38 par. Matt. 16.27) is also to be included in the last group.

(*a*) *The Father (without personal pronoun)*. The total number of instances are distributed as follows:

Mark	1[31]
Matthew and Luke together	—[32]
Additional instances peculiar to Luke	2[33]
Additional instances peculiar to Matthew	1[34]
John	73

The astonishing discrepancy in number between the Synoptics and John shows at a glance that ὁ πατήρ, used absolutely, was established as *the* designation for God only at a very late stage; the triadic baptismal formula in Matt. 28.19 suggests that the liturgy played an essential part in this process. Add to this the fact that of the five instances of ὁ πατήρ used absolutely in the Pauline writings (I Cor. 8.6; Rom. 6.4; Col. 1.12; Eph. 2.18; 3.14) the first occurs in a credal formula and the third and fifth in a prayer, and we have confirmation that as far as the early Christian practice of calling God 'Father' is concerned, the *lex orandi* determined the *lex credendi* (see above, p. 35). Of the four synoptic instances listed in the table above, Matt. 28.19 is to be discarded as a late liturgical formula, and the absolute ὁ πατήρ in Luke 9.26 goes back to a Lucan redaction of Mark 8.38. Thus only two passages remain to be examined for the possibility of traces of ancient tradition: Mark 13.32 and Luke 11.13.

In Mark 13.32 (περὶ δὲ τῆς ἡμέρας ἐκείνης ἢ τῆς ὥρας οὐδεὶς οἶδεν, οὐδὲ οἱ ἄγγελοι ἐν οὐρανῷ οὐδὲ ὁ υἱός, εἰ μὴ ὁ πατήρ) par. Matt. 24.36, ὁ υἱός and ὁ πατήρ, both used absolutely, stand side by side. ὁ υἱός used in this way is a christological title which became established rather late in the history of the early church: it occurs for the first time in Paul, but only once (I Cor. 15.28) and is used only

[31] Mark 13.32 par. Matt. 24.36.
[32] ὁ πατήρ, twice used absolutely in Matt. 11.27 par. Luke 10.22, does not belong in the list, as the article here is intended in a generic sense (see below, pp. 47f.).
[33] Luke 9.26; 11.13.   [34] Matt. 28.19.

rarely in subsequent decades (Matt. 28.19[35]; Heb. 1.8). Only in the Johannine literature[36] does it come to the fore. As ὁ υἱός used absolutely in this way as a title is not a designation for the Messiah in Palestinian linguistic usage,[37] Mark 13.32 can have reached its present form only in the context of the Hellenistic community.[38] If, however, we compare the passage with Acts 1.7, and venture the suggestion that οὐδὲ ὁ υἱός is an addition, then ὁ πατήρ in Mark 13.32 appears in a new light. The linguistic objections to ὁ υἱός do not arise in the case of ὁ πατήρ, as the corresponding word in Aramaic, אַבָּא, regularly meant 'my father' as well as 'the father'.[39] Thus if οὐδὲ ὁ υἱός may be regarded as an addition, Mark 13.32 is to be included among the 'my Father' sayings (see below, p. 52).

The second instance of ὁ πατήρ (without a personal pronoun) to be investigated occurs in Luke 11.13.

Luke 11.13:

πόσῳ μᾶλλον ὁ πατὴρ   ὁ ἐξ   οὐρανοῦ δώσει πνεῦμα ἅγιον τοῖς
αἰτοῦσιν αὐτόν

par. Matt. 7.11:

πόσῳ μᾶλλον ὁ πατὴρ ὑμῶν ὁ ἐν τοῖς οὐρανοῖς δώσει ἀγαθὰ   τοῖς
αἰτοῦσιν αὐτόν

The Matthaean version differs from the Lucan in having a ὑμῶν after the ὁ πατήρ. But this ὑμῶν is hardly original. If, as is probable,[40] this saying was addressed to the opponents of Jesus, 'your' is hardly appropriate, as the phrase 'your Father' is reserved for the disciples of Jesus in the earliest stratum of the tradition (see below, pp. 42f.). The phrase ὁ πατὴρ ὁ ἐξ οὐρανοῦ in Luke is striking; one

---

[35] Matt. 11.27 par. Luke 10.22 does not belong here, as in this passage the article before υἱός is meant in a generic sense (see below, pp. 46f.).

[36] 17 in the Gospel, 7 in the Epistles.

[37] There is evidence for the absolute use of הבן only as a designation for Israel (*Mek. Ex.* on 12.1).

[38] B. M. F. van Iersel, '*Der Sohn*' *in den synoptischen Jesusworten. Christusbezeichnung der Gemeinde oder Selbstbezeichnung Jesu?* (Supplements to NovT 3), Leiden 1961, regards 'the Son', in the absolute, at Mark 12.1-9 par., 13.32 and Matt. 11.27 par. to be authentic on the lips of Jesus. But he omits to examine Palestinian linguistic usage. Moreover, it is highly questionable whether one should appeal to Mark 12.1-9 (parable) and Matt. 11.27 par. (see below p. 46f.).

[39] See below, p. 58.

[40] J. Jeremias, *The Parables of Jesus*, ET², London 1963, pp. 144f. (following A. T. Cadoux).

would expect ἐν rather than ἐξ. This ἐξ is an instance of the attraction of a preposition as a result of the presence of δώσει; it is a classical usage, and there are also instances of it in the Septuagint[41] and the New Testament (Matt. 24.17; Col. 4.16). In view of the decided Hellenistic preference for periphrases with ἐκ,[42] we must assume that the author of the Lucan Vorlage himself used this attraction to demonstrate his literary education.[43] The flourish—and it is no more—does not in any way justify our taking the phrase ἐξ οὐρανοῦ with the verb (δώσει).[44] The preceding article makes that quite impossible. The qualification 'heavenly' also goes with ὁ πατήρ because of its content, and this is confirmed by Matthew: the contrast is not between earthly gifts and heavenly gifts, but between earthly fathers and the heavenly Father. The saying speaks of the heavenly Father (אבא דבשמיא) as the giver of 'good gifts' (so Matthew); these are not, however, the means of subsistence but the gifts of the age of salvation (in accordance with established eschatological linguistic usage).[45] The Lucan πνεῦμα ἅγιον is hardly original, but it has preserved this dimension. There is no reason at all to doubt that both the phrase אבא דבשמיא and the argument from the conduct of an earthly father to the love of God go back to Jesus himself (cf. Luke 15.11-32).

(b) *Your Father.* A survey of the evidence reveals the following distributions:

Mark	1[46]
Common to Matthew and Luke	2[47]
Additional instances peculiar to Luke	1[48]
Additional instances peculiar to Matthew	12[49]
John	2[50]

[41] W. F. Arndt – F. W. Gingrich – W. Bauer, *A Greek-English Lexicon of the New Testament*, Cambridge-Chicago 1957, p. 236.

[42] L. Radermacher, *Neutestamentliche Grammatik* (HNT 1)², Tübingen 1925, p. 26: 'thoroughly Hellenistic'.

[43] A. Schlatter, *Das Evangelium des Lukas*, Stuttgart 1931 = ²1960, p. 506.

[44] Against T. Zahn, *Das Evangelium des Lucas*³,⁴, Leipzig-Erlangen 1920, p. 454, n. 27; E. Klostermann, *Das Lukasevangelium* (HNT 5)², Tübingen 1929, p. 126 (as a possibility).

[45] Rom. 3.8; 10.15 (quoting Isa. 52.7 LXX); Heb. 9.11; 10.1; this connotation is also to be found in Luke 1.53.   [46] Mark 11.25.

[47] Matt. 5.48 (par. Luke 6.36); 6.32 (par. Luke 12.30).

[48] Luke 12.32.

[49] Matt. 5.16, 45; 6.1, 8, 14, 15, 26; 7.11; 10.20, 29; 18.14 (where the variant reading μου must be regarded as secondary, as μου was on the increase, see above, pp. 32f; μου will be an assimilation to 18.10, 19, 35); 23.9.

[50] John 8.42; 20.17.

Matthew again disturbs the pattern (see above, pp. 29f.). We need to be even more careful about the frequency of the instances in his writing $(2+12 = 14)$, as this time even John (only two instances) is against him. We do, however, have a means of control. We have synoptic parallels or comparable texts for no fewer than nine of the twelve passages (listed in n. 49) in which Matthew alone writes ὁ πατὴρ ὑμῶν: Matt. 5.45 (par. Luke 6.35); 6.8 (cf. Matt. 6.32 par. Luke 12.30), 14 (par. Mark 11.25), 15 (cf. Mark 11.25), 26 (par. Luke 12.24); 7.11 (par. Luke 11.13); 10.20 (par. Luke 12.12), 29 (par. Luke 12.6); 18.14 (par. Luke 15.7). Of these nine passages, comparable texts which also read 'your Father' can be found for only three (Matt. 6.8, 14, 15); the parallel to Matt. 7.11 (Luke 11.13) does indeed also speak of 'the Father', but it omits ὑμῶν, probably (as we saw above, pp. 37f.) rightly. In the remaining five instances (Matt. 5.45; 6.26; 10.20, 29; 18.14) the Lucan parallels have completely different designations for God[51]; both the ratio of instances in the table above and the fact that Matthew has twice replaced ὁ θεός with 'my Father' in his redaction of Mark (Matt. 12.50; 26.29) suggest that the Lucan parallels are more trustworthy in these five passages.[52] The remaining three passages of the twelve in which Matthew is the only one to have ὁ πατὴρ ὑμῶν (5.16; 6.1; 23.9) belong to his special material; but by analogy it seems by far the most probable explanation that here, too, the designation of God as 'Father' is secondary. Only in Matt. 23.9b is it firmly rooted in the text, and guaranteed by the protasis. So the majority of the Matthaean instances are to be regarded as secondary.

We should also leave on one side the two instances of ὁ πατὴρ ὑμῶν in the Fourth Gospel. John 20.17, a saying of the risen Christ, lies outside the scope of our investigation, which is limited to the earthly life of Jesus. John 8.42 is also to be excluded: while it is quite conceivable that Jesus denied his Jewish opponents the right to call God their Father, we have no synoptic parallels for the point of the conversation, that the devil, and not God, is their true father (ὁ πατὴρ ὑμῶν v. 41). One cannot appeal to the threat γεννήματα ἐχιδνῶν (Matt. 12.34; 23.33); ἐχιδνῶν is plural, and is not a periphrasis for the devil.

So once again the number of passages to be investigated has shrunk to a fraction of the original list.

Mark has 'your Father' in only one passage, in a saying which concludes the teaching on prayer which follows the pericope about the withered fig-tree: καὶ ὅταν στήκετε προσευχόμενοι,[53]

[51] Luke 6.35: ὕψιστος; 12.6, 24: ὁ θεός; 12.12: ἅγιον (πνεῦμα); 15.7: ἐν τῷ οὐρανῷ.
[52] Additional reasons for preferring the Lucan designations for God are: in the case of Luke 12.24 (par. Matt. 6.26), the context (see below, p. 40); in the case of Luke 15.7 (par. Matt. 18.14), a comparison with Luke 15.10; in the case of Luke 12.12 (par. Matt. 10.20), a comparison with Mark 13.11.
[53] These words of transition could come from Mark himself. He is the only synoptist to use στήκω (3.31; 11.25) and ὅταν with indicative (3.11 (summary); 11.19, 25; cf. Blass–Debrunner–Funk, §382.4).

ἀφίετε . . . ἵνα καὶ ὁ πατὴρ ὑμῶν ὁ ἐν τοῖς οὐρανοῖς ἀφῇ ὑμῖν (Mark 11.25). There is support for the phrase 'your heavenly Father' in passages with a parallel content, Matt. 6.14 ὁ πατὴρ ὑμῶν ὁ οὐράνιος[54] and 18.35 (here changed secondarily to ὁ πατὴρ μου ὁ οὐράνιος[55]). The saying is addressed to the disciples, as can be seen from its similarity to the petition for forgiveness in the Lord's Prayer.[56] The disciples must be ready to forgive if they are to pray rightly. God shows himself to be the Father of the disciples through his forgiveness.

There are only two passages in the whole of the sayings-material common to Matthew and Luke in which both gospels agree in having 'your Father' (see the table above). The first is Matt. 6.32 (οἶδεν γὰρ ὁ πατὴρ ὑμῶν ὁ οὐράνιος ὅτι χρῄζετε τούτων ἁπάντων) par. Luke 12.30 (ὑμῶν δὲ ὁ πατὴρ οἶδεν ὅτι χρῄζετε τούτων). Another tradition of the saying, in Matt. 6.8, which is quite independent from a literary point of view (οἶδεν γὰρ ὁ πατὴρ ὑμῶν ὧν χρείαν ἔχετε πρὸ τοῦ ὑμᾶς αἰτῆσαι αὐτόν), confirms the occurrence of the phrase 'your Father', as, above all, does the context. In the Lucan version the terminology changes to suit the content: ὁ θεός (Luke 12.24: God cares for the ravens), ὁ θεός (v. 28: God cares for the flowers) and then ὑμῶν δὲ ὁ πατήρ (v. 30; your Father cares for you). It is typical of Matthew that he destroys the symmetry and the climax of this triad; in his version, ὁ πατὴρ ὑμῶν ὁ οὐράνιος occurs in the very first passage, about the birds (6.26), ὁ θεός in the passage about the flowers (v. 30), and ὁ πατὴρ ὑμῶν ὁ οὐράνιος again in the case of the disciples (v. 32). The premature appearance of ὁ πατὴρ ὑμῶν ὁ οὐράνιος in Matthew at v. 26 is therefore secondary. On the other hand, ὁ πατὴρ ὑμῶν in v. 32 (par. Luke 12.30, cf. Matt. 6.8) seems to belong there. It is hardly a coincidence that this saying (like Mark 11.25, which we have just discussed) deals with prayer. God is called the Father of the disciples because he knows what they need before they ask him, and gives it to them.—The other passage in the sayings material in which Matthew and Luke agree in attesting the phrase 'your Father' is Matt. 5.48 (ἔσεσθε οὖν ὑμεῖς τέλειοι ὡς ὁ πατὴρ ὑμῶν ὁ οὐράνιος τέλειός ἐστιν) par. Luke 6.36 (γίνεσθε οἰκτίρμονες καθὼς ὁ πατὴρ ὑμῶν οἰκτίρμων ἐστίν). Here, the

---

[54] The antithesis at Matt. 6.15 has the shorter form ὁ πατὴρ ὑμῶν.
[55] See above, pp. 32f.
[56] For the Lord's Prayer as a prayer of the disciples see below, p. 53, n. 107, and pp. 63f.

Lucan οἰκτίρμων may well be original,[57] and the Matthaean τέλειος is probably a paraenetic generalization.[58] Once again, it is the goodness of God the Father which is stressed. Its boundlessness is to be a pattern for the disciples of Jesus and is to spur them on.

There is only one passage with 'your Father' in the special Lucan material, the word of comfort (12.32) which, taking up Dan. 7.27,[59] promises an eschatological change of fortune for the little flock. Its language is old.[60] In Dan. 7.27, the subject of the action appears only in a concealed form, in the passive; here, however, it is quite explicitly God the Father who gives the kingdom to the oppressed little flock. The reason for this difference may at least be that Jesus is speaking of a gift of God, the action which, next to his forgiveness, is most characteristic of his fatherly nature (cf. Matt. 7.11 par.).

Finally, we have one more passage to discuss, from the special Matthaean material[61]: 23.9 (καὶ πατέρα μὴ καλέσητε ὑμῶν ἐπὶ τῆς γῆς· εἷς γάρ ἐστιν ὑμῶν ὁ πατὴρ ὁ οὐράνιος).

The text of the first clause καὶ πατέρα μὴ καλέσητε ὑμῶν ἐπὶ τῆς γῆς, is difficult, because the second accusative which καλεῖν needs when it means 'address as, designate as' is not formally expressed. Μή has to be understood as μηδένα. A further difficulty is the uncertainty whether ὑμῶν is to be taken with πατέρα or with μή. Matt. 12.27 (αὐτοὶ κριταὶ ἔσονται ὑμῶν) would be relevant to the first possibility ('And you shall call no-one on earth your father'); here, too, the personal pronoun, placed afterwards, is separated by the verb from the word to which it refers. To support the second possibility ('And you shall call none of your number "father" on earth') one can refer to Acts 21.16 (συνῆλθον δὲ καὶ τῶν μαθητῶν) where the simple genitive (without ἐκ) is also used in a partitive sense.[62] The first instance would be a total prohibition against using the courtesy title 'father' at all (there is no question here of addressing a physical father); the second instance would be a partial prohibition: the disciples are to avoid the polite address 'father' only in

---

[57] Cf. *Targ. Jerus. I Lev.* 22.28 (Billerbeck I, p. 159), quoted above, p. 20; cf. n. 35 there.

[58] R. Schnackenburg, 'Die Vollkommenheit des Christen nach den Evangelien', *Theologisches Jahrbuch*, Leipzig 1961, pp. 71f.

[59] Δοῦναι τὴν βασιλείαν (Luke 12.32) = יהיבת.... מלכותה (Dan. 7.27).

[60] J. Jeremias, ποιμήν κτλ., *TWNT* VI (1959), p. 500, n. 20.

[61] We have already discussed four of the other eleven passages in which Matthew alone has 'your Father' (6.8 (see above, p. 40), 14, 15 (see above, pp. 39f.); 7.11 (see above, pp. 37f.)). For the remaining seven, see above, p. 39.

[62] F. Schulthess, 'Zur Sprache der Evangelien', *ZNW* 21 (1922), pp. 216-36, 241-58, here pp. 226f., also refers to LXX I Sam. 14.45; II Sam. 14.11; II Kings 10.23.

converse among themselves. E. Haenchen decides for the second translation and argues as follows: it is impossible that the disciples should have been regarded as teachers and have been addressed with the titles of Palestinian teachers of the law while Jesus was alive; but it *is* conceivable that Rabbis who attached themselves to the primitive community continued to claim their old titles of honour, like Rabbi, Abba. The community attacks such claims to titles in Matt. 23.8-10, verses which it created.[63] This presupposes that the addresses 'Rabbi' and 'Abba' were reserved for scholars. But this assumption is erroneous. 'Rabbi' ('my Lord') was *de facto* a polite form of address used quite generally in the first century AD, to Rabbis, among others[64]; but there are no examples of 'Abba' being used as a form of address to Rabbis.[65] It was rather used in conversation with old men.[66] Thus the limitation of the prohibition against using the courtesy title 'Abba' to the circle of the disciples (the second translation) is not to be explained by an influx of Rabbis into the primitive community and their desire for titles. There are two further considerations which go decisively against this limitation of the prohibition. First, $\dot{\epsilon}\pi\grave{\iota}\ \tau\hat{\eta}s\ \gamma\hat{\eta}s$ only makes sense in the context of a total prohibition such as we find with the first translation 'And you shall call no-one on earth your father'; $\dot{\epsilon}\pi\grave{\iota}\ \tau\hat{\eta}s\ \gamma\hat{\eta}s$ is to be taken with $\mu\acute{\eta}\ (=\mu\eta\delta\acute{\epsilon}\nu\alpha)$ and means 'no-one on earth', 'no man'. This all-embracing significance 'no man' cannot possibly be limited. Even if the contrast $\dot{\epsilon}\pi\grave{\iota}\ \tau\hat{\eta}s\ \gamma\hat{\eta}s\ /\ \acute{o}\ o\mathring{v}\rho\acute{\alpha}\nu\iota os$ was added later—and this could be quite conceivable in view of v. 8ab—the active $\mu\grave{\eta}\ \kappa\alpha\lambda\acute{\epsilon}\sigma\eta\tau\epsilon$ would go against a partial prohibition. This is the second consideration. If we recognize that Matt. 23.10 is secondary, formed by analogy with v. 8,[67] the progress of thought from the passive (v. 8: $\mu\grave{\eta}\ \kappa\lambda\eta\theta\hat{\eta}\tau\epsilon$) to the active (v. 9: $\mu\grave{\eta}\ \kappa\alpha\lambda\acute{\epsilon}\sigma\eta\tau\epsilon$) emerges clearly: the disciples are not to allow themselves to be called 'my lord' (say, by grateful people whom they have healed) (v. 8) and for their part they are to address no old man as 'my

---

[63] 'Matthäus 23', *ZTK* 48 (1951), pp. 42-5. Now too in *id.*, *Gott und Mensch. Gesammelte Aufsätze*, Tübingen 1965, pp. 33-6.

[64] G. Dalman, *The Words of Jesus I*, ET, Edinburgh 1902, p. 335.

[65] Dalman remarked as early as 1898 that 'We never find אַבָּא as an address

to a teacher', *op. cit.*, p. 339; similarly, Billerbeck I, p. 919.—*Siphre Deut.* 34 on 6.7: 'Thus just as the pupils are called sons, so the master is called father' is out of place here; as the context shows, the sentence merely states that in biblical terminology the nouns 'sons' and 'father' occur in a figurative sense.

[66] The earliest example from the first century BC (*b. Taʿan.* 23b), which has so far been passed over, is noted on p. 61 below: *j. Nidd.* 1.49b.42f.(Bar.): 'In the house of Rabban Gamaliel (II, *c.* AD 90) they called the slaves and maid-servants "Abba Ṭabhi, Imma Ṭabhitha"' (par. *b. Ber.* 16b (Bar.): 'Abba N. N., Imma N.N.'), though this address was prohibited for male and female slaves. Cf. further Ps.-Philo, *Liber antiquitatum biblicarum* 53.3 (Samuel addresses Eli as *pater*). There is a Hellenistic-Jewish example at IV Macc. 7.9.

[67] Matt. 23.10 is the only passage in the four gospels in which $\acute{o}\ X\rho\iota\sigma\tau\acute{o}s$ (with the article) occurs as a self-designation on the lips of the earthly Jesus (it occurs without the article at Mark 9.41; John 17.3, which are equally secondary).

father', because the honour of the name 'father' is to be reserved for God alone (v. 9). Just as it would be nonsense to limit the prohibition to the conversation of the disciples among themselves in the case of the passive (v. 8), because while the disciples addressed Jesus[68] as 'Rabbi' they did not use the title among themselves, so too, only the total prohibition makes any sense in the case of the active (v. 9).

'Call no man your father on earth, for you have one Father, who is in heaven.' The prohibition against the disciples' using the everyday, unexceptionable courtesy title 'Abba' loses its strangeness when we consider the unique way in which Jesus addressed God as 'Abba', a fact which is still to be discussed (see below, pp. 54ff.). This factor alone makes it possible to understand why Jesus protects the address 'Abba' from profanation. And that in turn means that in all probability the saying is authentic.

* * *

There are no serious reasons for disputing that any of the five 'your Father' sayings which we have just discussed go back to Jesus. He therefore spoke of God as 'your Father', though only to the disciples[69]; he never seems to have spoken of God as Father to outsiders except in parables and metaphors, never, at any rate, as 'your Father'.[70] 'Your Father' is thus one of the characteristic phrases in the *didache* given to the disciples. What content is associated with this phrase? God shows himself to be the Father of the disciples by forgiving them, visiting them with his tenderness and care, and preparing their salvation. The similarity between this and the use of the word 'Father' in the prophets is quite plain. But the new element should be stressed; the expressions of God's fatherly goodness are eschatological events (cf. Matt. 7.11 par.; Luke 12.32).

---

[68] Mark 9.5; 11.21; 14.45 (par. Matt. 26.49); Matt. 26.25; John 4.31; 9.2; 11.8.

[69] This is supported by John 20.17 and also 8.42, where in a dispute Jesus denies the Jews the right to call God their Father: εἰ ὁ θεὸς πατὴρ ὑμῶν ἦν, ἠγαπᾶτε ἂν ἐμέ.

[70] Most recently, H. W. Montefiore, 'God as Father in the Synoptic Gospels', *NTS* 3 (1956-7), pp. 31-46, has attempted to demonstrate that Jesus nevertheless taught the 'Universal Fatherhood' of God (most clearly in the 'Father' sayings in the Sermon on the Mount). Montefiore's work suffers from two basic weaknesses: he does not pose the question of authenticity radically enough, and he asks whether the idea of the universal Fatherhood of God can be reconciled with the texts, instead of first interpreting them within the framework of Jesus' sayings about the Father.

(c) *My Father*.   Once again, a survey of the material:

Mark	1(?)[71]
Common to Matthew and Luke	1[72]
Additional instances peculiar to Luke	3[73]
Additional instances peculiar to Matthew	13[74]
John	25

The way in which the number of instances increases once again warns us to be careful in Matthew, and even more so in John. There is confirmation of the need for this care in the fact that Matthew has twice replaced ὁ θεός in the Marcan text (3.35; 14.25) with 'my (heavenly) Father' (Matt. 12.50; 26.29) and that he has added ὑπὸ τοῦ πατρός μου to Mark 10.40 on his own initiative (Matt. 20.23). Under these circumstances, one will certainly prefer the Lucan versions in the parallels to Matt. 7.21 (par. Luke 6.46) and 10.32f. (par. Luke 12.8f.), in neither of which does 'my heavenly Father' occur. Two further Matthaean passages may be left out of account for other reasons. In Matt. 18.35, 'my Father' corresponds with a 'your Father' in passages with a similar content (Mark 11.25; Matt. 6.14f.); in such cases, as we saw on p. 33 above, 'your Father' has the claim to priority. Moreover, if Matt. 18.10 was originally addressed to Jesus' adversaries, as the μὴ καταφρονήσατε might suggest, one would not expect God to be called 'my heavenly Father' here; so this instance, too, will not belong to the oldest tradition. Of the five remaining instances of 'my (heavenly) Father' peculiar to Matthew (15.13; 16.17; 18.19; 25.34; 26.53), 16.17 has the greatest claim to originality because of the similarity of its content to 11.27 (par. Luke 10.22).

We must also disregard Mark 8.38, where it is said of the Son of Man: ὅταν ἔλθῃ ἐν τῇ δόξῃ τοῦ πατρὸς αὐτοῦ μετὰ τῶν ἀγγέλων τῶν ἁγίων. In this saying the ἐνώπιον τῶν ἀγγέλων (without τοῦ θεοῦ!) of Luke 12.9 is probably original. This conclusion is supported by the pre-Matthaean tradition, which also introduces the name 'Father' elsewhere (see below, pp. 30f.); it says ἔμπροσθεν τοῦ πατρός μου τοῦ ἐν οὐρανοῖς (Matt. 10.33). The ὅταν clause in Mark 8.38 looks like a combination of these two phrases.—On the other hand, Mark 13.32 par. Matt. 24.36 (ὁ πατήρ) is to be added to the instances of 'my Father' given in the table above, if, as suggested on p. 37, οὐδὲ ὁ υἱός may be regarded as an addition, and the absolute ὁ πατήρ corresponds to an 'Abba' in the sense of 'my father'.

Of the three passages from the Lucan special material (2.49; 22.29; 24.49), the first belongs to the infancy narratives and the third to the

---

[71] Mark 8.38 par. Matt. 16.27: τοῦ πατρὸς αὐτοῦ, viz. of the Son of Man. This passage can only be included among the instances of 'my Father' with reservations.

[72] Matt. 11.27 par. Luke 10.22.   [73] Luke 2.49; 22.29; 24.49.

[74] Matt. 7.21; 10.32f.; 12.50; 15.13; 16.17; 18.10, 19, 35; 20.23; 25.34; 26.29, 53.

resurrection stories; neither of them therefore falls within the scope of our investigation.

So only four passages in all remain for us to examine: Mark 13.32 (par. Matt. 24.36); Matt. 11.27 (par. Luke 10.22); Matt. 16.17; Luke 22.29.

The authenticity of the saying Matt. 11.27 par. Luke 10.22

We shall begin with Matt. 11.27 (par. Luke 10.22).[75] First of all, something should be said about the age of the tradition.

Karl von Hase, who in the last century was professor of church history at Jena, in his book on the life of Jesus coined the famous simile that this synoptic saying 'gives the impression of a thunderbolt fallen from the Johannine sky'.[76] Two things above all in this text appeared Johannine: first, the phrase about mutual knowledge which was regarded as a technical term drawn from Hellenistic mysticism, and second, the designation of Jesus as ὁ υἱός, which is characteristic of Johannine christology (Gospel 15 times, Epistles 8 times). Before John, this absolute ὁ υἱός, with the article, occurs only at I Cor. 15.28; Mark 13.32 par. Matt. 24.36; Matt. 28.19; Heb. 1.8. Moreover, the use of the absolute ὁ πατήρ as a title for God is, as we saw on p. 33 above, almost a hallmark of the Johannine writings.

These objections have been repeated constantly. For a long time it was considered certain that Matt. 11.27 par. was a late product of Hellenistic Christianity.[77] In the last decades, however, the tide has begun to turn.[78] The objections mentioned above are in fact quite untenable. The explicitly semitic character of the saying, which is clear both from its language and its style, tells against the description of it as a 'Hellenistic revelation saying'.[79]

---

[75] Literature in Schrenk, *op. cit.*, p. 993, n. 228, and in F. Hahn, *Christologische Hoheitstitel. Ihre Geschichte im frühen Christentum* (FRLANT 83), Göttingen 1963 = ²1964, pp. 321-30.

[76] K. A. von Hase, *Die Geschichte Jesu²*, Leipzig 1876, p. 422.

[77] Thus, though formulated very carefully ('redaction of authentic words of Jesus'), even Schrenk, *op. cit.*, p. 994.

[78] English scholars, in particular, have protested strongly here. T. W. Manson, *The Sayings of Jesus*, London 1949 = 1950 (1937¹), p. 79: 'The passage is full of Semitic turns of phrase, and certainly Palestinian in origin'; *id.*, *The Teaching of Jesus²*, Cambridge 1935 = 1948, pp. 109-12; W. L. Knox, *Some Hellenistic Elements in Primitive Christianity* (Schweich Lectures 1942), London 1944, p. 7: 'If we reject it, it must be on the grounds of our general attitude to the person of Jesus, not on the ground that its form or language are "hellenistic" in any intelligible sense.'

[79] R. Bultmann, *The History of the Synoptic Tradition*, ET, Oxford 1963, p. 159.

Vocabulary: οὐδείς | εἰ μή, or οὐδέ | εἰ μή corresponds to a לֵית | אֶלָּא

(typically Aramaic[80] paraphrase for 'only'); the meaning 'reveal' for ἀποκαλύπτειν is not Greek.[81] Semitic *style* is to be seen in the asyndeton at the beginning; in the repetition of the verb in the second and third lines, which Greek taste found ugly (Luke therefore avoided it); in the synthetic parallelism of the second and third lines which serves to replace the defective reciprocal pronoun (see below); and in the structure of the four line stanza which is exactly paralleled in Matt. 11.25f.: both four line stanzas mention the theme first, in line 1, then elaborate it with two parallel clauses in the second and third lines, the second line being subordinate to the third, despite the formal parataxis in each case (see below), and end in the fourth line with an emphatic last clause. Finally, the *differences* between Matt. 11.27 and the parallel version in Luke 10.22 should be noted: in the second line Luke has the simple γινώσκει (Matt.: ἐπιγινώσκει) and has an indirect question in the second and third lines instead of the object; he has καί at the beginning of the third line (Matt. οὐδέ) and, as has been remarked above, avoids repeating the verb. This last divergence is likely to be a stylistic correction by Luke. On the other hand, the καί at the beginning of the third line cannot be attributed to Luke's editing, as Luke cuts down on the frequent use of καί in his material[82] and never alters an οὐδέ in the text of Mark to καί. So at least in this καί we have a variant tradition or translation; in the latter case it would be a pointer to an Aramaic original underlying both versions. The only strange point is the introduction of the subject with ὑπό after a passive (παρεδόθη). This is not impossible for Palestinian Aramaic, but it is unusual,[83] and to be regarded as a Graecism.

Language, style and structure thus clearly assign the saying to a Semitic-speaking milieu. The two arguments for an allegedly Hellenistic origin mentioned initially ('mystical' knowledge and the use of ὁ υἱός and ὁ πατήρ as titles) can be answered on linguistic grounds. True, Hellenistic mysticism and Gnosticism offer expressions similar to the contrast of (ἐπι)γινώσκειν used twice in the active (Matt. 11.27 par. Luke 10.22: lines 2 and 3), but so far no exact parallel has been indicated in this context. I shall shortly draw attention to an exact formal analogy in the book of Tobit,

[80] K. Beyer, *Semitische Syntax im Neuen Testament*, I 1 (SUNT 1), Göttingen 1962, p. 105.

[81] A. Oepke, καλύπτω κτλ., *TWNT* III (1938), p. 568.19f. (Cf. on the other hand in Judaism: Sirach 3.19: Hebrew ולענוים יגלה סודו, LXX πραέσιν ἀποκαλύπτει τὰ μυστήρια αὐτοῦ.)

[82] H. J. Cadbury, *The Style and Literary Method of Luke* (Harvard Theological Studies 6), Cambridge 1920, pp. 142f.

[83] G. Dalman, *The Words of Jesus*, I, *ET*, Edinburgh 1902, p. 284, n. 1.

which has not yet been noticed, as far as I am aware. So it can no longer be said that while 'the idea of such mutual knowledge cannot be excluded' in Judaism, there are 'no actual examples'.[84] Such contrasts with verbal repetition are idiomatic semitic usage. What seems to us to be a roundabout way of expression is a common device for expressing a reciprocal relationship. As semitic languages lack a reciprocal pronoun ('one another', 'each other'), they either have to help themselves out with periphrases (e.g. איש אחיו = ἀλλήλους, cf. Matt. 18.35 ἕκαστος τῷ ἀδελφῷ αὐτοῦ) or take refuge in repetitions, as for example: 'the first will receive the last . . . and the last those whom they have heard to have gone before them' (for: first and last will receive each other)[85] or: 'these agree with those and those agree with these' (for: they agree together)[86] or: 'these gave reasons for their views and those gave reasons for their views' (for: each gave the other their reasons),[87] or a quite striking parallel to the present logion:

αὐτὸς οὐ γινώσκει με
καὶ ἐγὼ οὐ γινώσκω αὐτόν

(for: we do not know each other).[88] As G. Dalman recognized,[89] Matt. 11.27 is an exact parallel; the monotony of the parallel lines

οὐδεὶς ἐπιγινώσκει τὸν υἱὸν εἰ μὴ ὁ πατήρ,
οὐδὲ τὸν πατέρα τις ἐπιγινώσκει εἰ μὴ ὁ υἱός

is simply an oriental periphrasis for a mutual relationship: only father and son really know each other.

This also does away with the second objection, that the use of ὁ υἱός and ὁ πατήρ in the absolute shows that Matt. 11.27 is Hellenistic. If Matt. 11.27 has nothing to do with Hellenistic mysticism, but rather belongs in a Semitic-speaking milieu (see above p. 45), then we are not to understand ὁ υἱός as a title; for there are no instances of ὁ υἱός being used in the absolute as a Messianic title either in ancient Judaism[90] or in the pre-Hellenistic strata of the New Testament. In the light of semitic linguistic usage, the articles before υἱός and before πατήρ are to be under-

---

[84] Hahn, *op. cit.*, p. 324. [85] Syr. Bar. 51.13 (Violet).
[86] *j. Rosh. Hash.* 2.58b.20f. (noted by Dalman, *op. cit.*, p. 283, n. 1).
[87] *Gen.* R. 1.21 on 1.1.
[88] Tobit 5.2א; cf. also Test. Naph. 7.3 (Jacob, about Joseph): οὐ βλέπω σε, καὶ σὺ οὐχ ὁρᾷς Ἰακὼβ τὸν γεννήσαντά σε (references from Dr C. Burchard).
[89] Dalman, *op. cit.*, p. 283. [90] See above, p. 37.

stood in a generic sense.[91] Thus Matt. 11.27b-d was originally
meant as a statement of general experience. There is a completely
analogous statement of general experience, also concerned with
the father-son relationship, in John 5.19-20a, if C. H. Dodd is
right. He believes that this passage is 'une parabole cachée', i.e.
that it was originally an everyday metaphor of the son as his
father's pupil.[92] (That the evangelists understood ὁ υἱός as a title
both in Matt. 11.27 par. Luke 10.22 and in John 5.19-20a is quite
another question; we are here concerned with the original sense
of the sayings.)

One final word about the allegedly 'Johannine' ring of this
passage. It would be quite unparalleled if a Johannine logion had
found its way into the synoptic corpus. Moreover, the fact that
both ἐπιγινώσκειν (so Matthew) and ἀποκαλύπτειν are not Johannine
words tells against this assumption; ἐπιγινώσκειν does not occur at
all in the Johannine writings, and ἀποκαλύπτειν occurs only once,
in a quotation from the LXX (John 12.38, quoting Isa. 53.1 LXX).
Nor is παραδιδόναι used with God as subject in John, as it is in
Matt. 11.27 par. On the other hand, we can easily understand how,
once the absolute ὁ υἱός was taken as a title, this passage could
have been an important stimulus to Johannine christology and its
remarks about knowledge (cf. John 10.15). Indeed, without such
points of departure in the synoptic tradition it would be an
eternal puzzle how Johannine theology could have originated at
all.

If, then, there is nothing against the authenticity of our logion,
the intrinsic connection it has with the way in which Jesus
addressed God as 'Abba' is decisively in its favour.

The meaning of the saying Matt. 11.27 par. Luke 10.22

The exegesis of the saying must begin from its structure.[93]
It is a four-line stanza:

[91] See e.g. H. F. W. Gesenius – E. Kautzsch – A. E. Cowley, *Hebrew Grammar*, ET², Oxford 1910, §126 *l*.

[92] C. H. Dodd, 'Une parabole cachée dans le quatrième Evangile', *RHPR* 42 (1962), pp. 107-15; this was seen at the same time, and apparently independently of Dodd, by P. Gaechter, 'Zur Form von Joh. 5,19-30', in: J. Blinzler – O. Kuss – F. Mussner, *Neutestamentliche Aufsätze* (J. Schmid Festschrift), Regensburg 1963, pp. 65-8, here p. 67.

[93] Like D. F. Strauss before him, E. Norden, *Agnostos Theos*, Berlin 1913 = ²1923 = Darmstadt 1956, pp. 277-308, wanted to see Matt. 11.25-30 as an original unity; he pointed out that Sirach 51.1-30 had an analogous structure

1. Πάντα μοι παρεδόθη ὑπὸ τοῦ πατρός μου,
2. καὶ οὐδεὶς ἐπιγινώσκει τὸν υἱὸν εἰ μὴ ὁ πατήρ,
3. οὐδὲ τὸν πατέρα τις ἐπιγινώσκει εἰ μὴ ὁ υἱὸς
4. καὶ ᾧ ἐὰν βούληται ὁ υἱὸς ἀποκαλύψαι.   (Matt. 11.27)

The Lucan version (10.22), which differs only slightly, shows faint signs of Greek influence in the omission of the verb in the third line.

As we have seen, the first line introduces the theme: 'My Father has[94] given me all things.' Matt. 28.18 should not mislead us into supposing that πάντα refers to lordly power; this would not fit the context of vv. 25f. and 27b-d, where only the revelation of God is mentioned. As παραδιδόναι (= מסר) is used as a technical term for the transmission of doctrine, knowledge and holy lore,[95] πάντα refers to knowledge of God, just as ταῦτα in v. 25 designates the mystery of revelation. Thus in v.27a, Jesus is saying: God has given me a full revelation.

The second line (καὶ οὐδεὶς ἐπιγινώσκει τὸν υἱὸν εἰ μὴ ὁ πατήρ) seems at first sight to be completely irrelevant to its context, which is simply concerned with knowledge of God (and not of the son!). This apparent break in the train of thought has led to the deletion or transposition of the second line, right up to modern times.[96] But to do this is completely to misunderstand the structure of the saying. As in Matt. 11.25f., which has a similar structure, the clause which gives the theme of Matt. 11.27 is followed by two lines, linked in parallelism, which elaborate it:

---

and argued that in both passages we have the same type of religious propaganda. But neither Sirach 51.1-30 nor Matt. 11.25-30 originally formed a unity. Sirach 51.1-12 is a hymn of thanksgiving to which an alphabetical acrostic has been attached (vv. 13-30). The unity of Matt. 11.25-30 is equally doubtful. Luke does not have vv. 28-30, and although the two remaining four-line stanzas (vv. 25f. and v. 27) have the same structure, it is questionable whether they originally belonged together, because Luke has his own introduction to each of them (Luke 10.21, 22); they may have been connected by catchword association, because ἀποκαλύπτειν occurs in each of them.

[94] I have translated this in the active, as the passive is a periphrasis for the action of God.

[95] J. Jeremias, *The Eucharistic Words of Jesus*, ET², London 1966, pp. 101, 202.

[96] See most recently P. Winter, 'Matthew XI 27 and Luke X 22 from the First to the Fifth Century', *NovT* 1 (1956), pp. 122-48, here especially pp. 129-34.

καὶ οὐδεὶς ἐπιγινώσκει τὸν υἱὸν εἰ μὴ ὁ πατήρ,
οὐδὲ τὸν πατέρα τις ἐπιγινωσκει εἰ μὴ ὁ υἱός.

In these two lines, we have a formal parataxis combined with a
logical hypotaxis.[97] We can see this most clearly from v. 25bc.
The thanksgiving in v. 25 is not about the concealment of knowledge, but about its revelation. So Matt. 11.25 must be translated
with the second line subordinate to the third:

(I thank thee)
that while thou hast hidden these things from the wise and understanding, thou hast revealed them to babes.

In v. 27, the second line is subordinated in just the same way to
the third, which has the emphasis (weight at the end). Add to this
the fact that, as we saw on pp. 47f. above, ὁ υἱός and ὁ πατήρ are to
be understood generically, the two parallel lines in v. 27bc making
a picture from everyday life, and to match the sense we should
translate:

Just as only a father really knows his son,
so only a son really knows his father.

The correctness of this translation is confirmed by John 10.15:

καθὼς γινώσκει με ὁ πατὴρ
κἀγὼ γινώσκω τὸν πατέρα.

The final line (καὶ ᾧ ἐὰν βούληται ὁ υἱὸς ἀποκαλύψαι) continues the
imagery (ὁ υἱός is again to be understood generically) and follows
on smoothly from what precedes it: because only a son really
knows his father, he alone is in a position to pass this knowledge
on to others.

Now it is important to realize that the father-son comparison is
used in Palestinian apocalyptic as an illustration of how revelation
is transmitted. Here are some examples. 'Every secret did I (God)
reveal to him (*Meṭaṭron*) as a father' (*Hebrew* [III] *Enoch* 48C.7).
'Rabbi Ishmael said: *Meṭaṭron* said to me: Come, I will show you
the curtain of God which is drawn before the Holy One (blessed
be He), on which all the generations of the world and all their
doings . . . are woven. (2) And I went, and he showed me with
the fingers of his hands—like a father who is teaching his son the
letters of the Torah' (*Hebrew Enoch* 45.1f. MS E). The metaphor of

[97] Norden, *op. cit.*, pp. 286f.

the son as the pupil of his father, understood in its original sense,[98] also belongs here: 'Truly, truly, I say to you: a son can do nothing of his own accord, (but) only what he sees his father doing; for whatever he does, his son does likewise. For a father loves his son, and shows him all that he himself is doing' (John 5.19-20a).

Thus, in interpreting the theme 'The Father has transmitted all things to me' with the aid of this father-son comparison, what Jesus wants to convey in the guise of an everyday simile is this: Like a father who personally devotes himself to explaining the letters of the Torah to his son, like a father who initiates a son into the well-preserved secrets of his craft, so God has transmitted to me the revelation of himself, and therefore I alone can pass on to others the real knowledge of God.

Matt. 11.27 is a key statement by Jesus about his mission. But it does not stand isolated in the gospels. There are numerous parallels[99] in the gospels to the consciousness of being in a singular way the recipient and mediator of knowledge of God which is expressed in Matt. 11.27: Mark 4.11 (Jesus passes on the μυστήριον τῆς βασιλείας τοῦ θεοῦ); Matt. 11.25 (Jesus possesses and teaches ταῦτα; God reveals it through him); Luke 10.23f. (the disciples can see and hear what has not been granted to prophets and kings); Matt. 5.17 (Jesus brings the final revelation); Luke 15.1-7, 8-10, 11-32 (Jesus' actions reflect God's attitude to sinners), etc.[100]

According to a special tradition, Matt. 11.26 also belongs here.[101] The Gnostic sect of the Marcosians handed down Matt. 11.26 in the following version[102]:

οὐά, ὁ πατήρ μου, ὅτι ἔμπροσθέν σου εὐδοκία μοι ἐγένετο.

This form of the saying undoubtedly goes back to an Aramaic tradition. The evidence for this is: (a) οὐά = רֵּי = Oh! is an Aramaic exclamation

---

[98] See above, pp. 47f.

[99] Cf. L. Cerfaux, 'La connaissance des secrets du Royaume d'après Matt. XIII 11 et parallèles', *NTS* 2 (1955-6), pp. 242f.

[100] G. Jeremias, *Der Lehrer der Gerechtigkeit* (SUNT 2), Göttingen 1963, pp. 319ff., esp. pp. 327f., 336ff.

[101] A. Merx, *Das Evangelium Matthaeus nach der syrischen im Sinaikloster gefundenen Palimpsesthandschrift* (Die vier kanonischen Evangelien nach ihrem ältesten bekannten Texte II 1), Berlin 1902, p. 200. For what follows see W. Grundmann, *Die Geschichte Jesu Christi*, Berlin 1957, p. 80 and n. 1.; *id.*, 'Die νήπιοι in der urchristlichen Paränese', *NTS* 5 (1958-9), pp. 202f.

[102] Text in Irenaeus, *Haer.* I 13.2.

of triumphant joy; (*b*) The vocative ὁ πατήρ μου is a rendering of אַבָּא;
(*c*) μοι ἐγένετο = הָוָה לִי is semitic; moreover, ἐγένετο is a paraphrase
for the action of God; (*d*) the Marcosians have the plural τῶν οὐρανῶν
at the beginning of the cry of joy in contrast to the singular τοῦ οὐρανοῦ
of Matt. 11.25 par. Luke 10.21. So according to the tradition of the
Marcosians, the cry of Jesus ran:

'O my Father, that good pleasure was granted me before thee!'
According to this ancient variant, Jesus counted himself among the
νήπιοι mentioned immediately beforehand in Matt. 11.25 par. Luke
10.21. He rejoices that he is the νήπιος of God, his beloved child, to
whom the revelation has been given. Even though this variant form of
the tradition of Matt. 11.26 is secondary, it strikes the original note of
Jesus' joy over the revelation granted to him, a joy which also per-
meates the present text.

We do not know when and where Jesus received the revelation
in which God allowed him to participate in complete divine
knowledge—as a father allows his son to share in knowledge.
The aorist indicates one particular experience. Perhaps we should
think of the baptism.

The remaining passages

We need spend little time on the remaining passages in which
Jesus calls God his Father. Matt. 16.17 (σὰρξ καὶ αἷμα οὐκ ἀπεκάλυψέν
σοι ἀλλ᾽ ὁ πατήρ μου ἐν τοῖς οὐρανοῖς) is closely related to Matt. 11.27
par.; here, too, 'my Father' is spoken in the context of the self-
revelation of God. Mark 13.32 stands equally close to Matt. 11.27
par. Here, however, the extent of the revelation is said to be
limited—an indication of considerable antiquity: only the Father
is omniscient.[103] Luke 22.29 (διέθετό μοι ὁ πατήρ μου βασιλείαν)
takes up Dan. 7.14: לֵהּ יְהִיב שָׁלְטָן וִיקָר וּמַלְכוּ. βασιλεία without
the article in Luke 22.29 designates the kingly might (not the
realm) which Jesus is promised by his Father. Luke 22.29 is also
close to Matt. 11.27; to the present gift of the Father, revelation, is
added the promise of his future gift: royal estate.

*   *   *

All the 'my Father' sayings we have discussed deal with the
unique revelation and authority which have been given to Jesus.
In the earliest stratum, they are strictly limited to the specific

---

[103] If οὐδὲ ὁ υἱός may be regarded as an addition (see above, p. 37), there is
nothing to prevent us seeing an old tradition in Mark 13.32.

relationship of Jesus to God.[104] The sparseness of the instances in the earliest stratum of the tradition shows that Jesus did not often speak of the ultimate mystery of his mission, and their limitation to words addressed to the disciples shows that they belong to the esoteric teaching of Jesus.[105] In his public preaching, Jesus clarified the nature and action of God in parables about the conduct of an earthly father[106]; he kept the direct designation of God as 'my Father' for his teaching to the disciples. The esoteric teaching is indeed the reason for the selection of the group of disciples.[107]

Jesus bases his authority on the fact that God has revealed himself to him like a father to his son. 'My Father' is thus a word of revelation. It represents the central statement of Jesus' mission. In making Jesus' communion with the Father and the authority based on it the central point of Jesus' message, the Gospel of John has preserved a historical fact, despite the way in which it has increased the number of instances and despite its ignorance of the way in which the message was limited to the group of disciples.

There is nothing in Rabbinic literature which corresponds to this use of 'my Father' by Jesus. The two Tannaitic instances of the phrase 'my heavenly Father' cited on pp. 18 and 22 above are of a different kind. They apply to all Israelites, or to all Israelites involved in persecution, and therefore apply quite generally, whereas 'my Father' on the lips of Jesus expresses a unique

[104] This can also be seen in the way in which Jesus never associates himself with the disciples in the phrase 'our Father', not even in the Lord's Prayer, where the shorter form of address ($\pi \acute{a} \tau \epsilon \rho$ Luke 11.2) is original. Cf. 'The Lord's Prayer', below, pp. 85-93.

[105] This was first recognized by T. W. Manson, *The Teaching of Jesus*[2], Cambridge 1935 = 1948, p. 102.

[106] Luke 15.11-32; Matt. 7.9-11 par. Luke 11.11-13 etc.

[107] In objecting that: 'In my opinion, Abba should not be taken as a mark of Jesus' esoteric teaching; this is impossible, simply by virtue of the Lord's Prayer', F. Hahn, *Christologische Hoheitstitel* (FRLANT 83), Göttingen 1963 = [2]1964, p. 320, n.3, fails to understand that the Lord's Prayer is a prayer for the disciples. It was not reserved for the baptised only at a later stage in the ancient church; this also happened at an early period, as can be seen from the structure of the Didache: pre-baptismal instruction (1-6) is followed by baptism (7), and only then do the Lord's prayer (8) and the Lord's supper (9-10) follow. Cf. T. W. Manson, 'The Lord's Prayer', *BJRL* 38 (1955-6), pp. 101f., and below, pp. 83f. In view of the numerous references to baptism in I Peter, it has frequently been conjectured that I Peter 1.17 ($\epsilon \grave{\iota} \pi a \tau \acute{\epsilon} \rho a \, \acute{\epsilon} \pi \iota \kappa a \lambda \epsilon \hat{\iota} \sigma \theta \epsilon \, \tau \grave{o} \nu \ldots$) refers to the tradition of the Lord's Prayer at baptism. This is illuminating. For the Lord's Prayer as a prayer of the disciples, see further pp. 63f.

relationship with God.[108] If we are looking for any prefigurements we must go back to the Old Testament, and recall the prophecy of Nathan, which promises to the descendant of David: 'I will be his father, and he shall be my son' (II Sam. 7.14 par. I Chron. 17.13), and to the words about the king in Ps. 2.7; 89.26.[109]

[108] H. Braun, *Spätjüdisch-häretischer und frühchristlicher Radikalismus*, II (Beiträge zur historischen Theologie 24 II), Tübingen 1957, p. 127, n. 2, has challenged this by remarking that we 'do in fact have three Rabbinic passages which refer to "my Father" '. But he overlooks two things: (1), that the two Tannaitic examples, as has been pointed out above in the text, have a general application, and (2) that the third instance produced by Braun from Billerbeck I, p. 394, in which R. Zadok (AD 50-80) is said to have addressed God as 'my heavenly Father', is a historically worthless anachronism, as it derives from a writing produced in South Italy in the tenth century (see above, p. 28 on the *Seder Eliyyahu Rabbah*).

[109] The promise given to the priestly Messiah that God will speak to him with 'the voice of a father' (Test. Levi 18.6) and the promise to the Messiah of Judah that the 'blessing of the holy Father' will be poured out on him (Test. Juda 24.2) are both suspect of being due to Christian influence.

B. *'Father' as an address in the prayers of Jesus*

(i) *The tradition*

The result of the above investigation of the sayings of Jesus is confirmed and becomes even more profound when we turn to his prayers. We now move on from the *designation* of God as Father in the words of Jesus to the *addressing* of God as Father in his prayers.

All five strata of the Gospel tradition agree that Jesus addressed God as Father in prayer. The instances are distributed as follows:

Mark	1[1]
Common to Matthew and Luke	3[2]
Additional instances peculiar to Luke	2[3]
Additional instances peculiar to Matthew	1[4]
John	9[5]

A critical scrutiny of the instances shows that the earliest layer of tradition is represented by the Lord's Prayer (in the Lucan

[1] Mark 14.36 (par. Matt. 26.39; Luke 22.42).
[2] Matt. 6.9 (par. Luke 11.2); 11.25, 26 (par. Luke 10.21ab).
[3] Luke 23.34, 46.
[4] Matt. 26.42 (repetition of 26.39 par. Mark 14.36).
[5] John 11.41; 12.27f.; 17.1, 5, 11, 21, 24, 25, two of these with an adjectival attribute: 17.11 ($\pi\acute{a}\tau\epsilon\rho$ $\ddot{a}\gamma\iota\epsilon$), 25 ($\pi\acute{a}\tau\epsilon\rho$ $\delta\acute{\iota}\kappa\alpha\iota\epsilon$).

version),[6] the cry of jubilation, which is thoroughly semitic both in language and style (Matt. 11.25f. par. Luke 10.21), and the prayer in Gethsemane with its address 'Abba' (Mark 14.36). This does not, however, rob the other instances of their value. For only if one takes them into consideration does a most significant fact become clear: not only do the five strata agree that Jesus did in fact use the address 'Father', but they are also at one in making Jesus use this address in *all* his prayers, with one exception. The cry from the cross, Mark 15.34 par. Matt. 27.46, is: 'My God, my God, why hast thou forsaken me?' Here the form of address 'my God' was supplied by the text of the psalm quoted. This constancy of the tradition shows how firmly the address 'Father' was rooted in the tradition of Jesus, quite apart from the question of the authenticity of the individual prayers themselves.

It is still more significant that we see that Jesus used the Aramaic word אַבָּא (accent on the final syllable)[7] when he addressed God as Father. While this occurs explicitly in the Gospels only at Mark 14.36, two other points confirm it. First, we should remember that the primitive church also addressed God as 'Abba'; Paul bears witness to this not only in the case of the communities in Galatia, which he founded (Gal. 4.6), but also in the case of the Roman church, which was still unknown to him (Rom. 8.15). This quite striking use of an alien Aramaic word in the prayer of the Greek-speaking communities goes back to the example of Jesus, as is certainly shown by the uniqueness of the linguistic usage.[8] This presupposes that Jesus frequently used 'Abba' as a form of address to God. Secondly, the variation in the form of the vocative between πάτερ,[9] πάτερ μου,[10] ὁ πατήρ[11] and πατήρ[12] should also be noted.

These variations occur at different levels. The use of the nomi-

[6] See 'The Lord's Prayer', pp. 89-94.

[7] With very few exceptions, Galilean Aramaic has the stress on the last syllable.

[8] See below, pp. 57ff.

[9] Matt. 11.25 par. Luke 10.21; Luke 11.2; 22.42; 23.34, 46; John 11.41; 12.27, 28; 17.1, 5, 11, 21, 24, 25.

[10] Matt. 26.39, 42.

[11] Mark 14.36; Matt. 11.26 par. Luke 10.21; Rom. 8.15; Gal. 4.6.

[12] John 17.5 D* 11 B ℵ, 21 BDW *pc*, 24 BA *pc*, 25 BA *pc*. K. Aland (in: E. Nestle-K. Aland, *Novum Testamentum Graece*[25], Stuttgart 1963; *Synopsis Quattuor Evangeliorum*, Stuttgart 1964) takes πάτερ to be the original reading in John 17.1, 5, 11 and πατήρ in vv. 21, 24, 25. The latter can hardly be right.

native πατήρ without the article as a form of address is a piece of vulgarity ('scribal *faux-pas*').[13] It comes about, as the papyri show, by the occasional suppression of the special vocative form in the third declension by the nominative (πατήρ, μήτηρ, θυγάτηρ) in popular usage.[14] The variation of the manuscripts between πάτερ and πατήρ (John 17.5, 11, 21, 24f.) is thus a variation purely within the Greek, like their variation between θύγατερ and θυγάτηρ (Matt. 9.22; Mark 5.34; Luke 8.48; John 12.15). The variation between πάτερ, ὁ πατήρ and πάτερ μου is a different matter. The use of the nominative with the article as a vocative in addressing God (ὁ πατήρ Mark 14.36; Matt. 11.26 par. Luke 10.21; Rom. 8.15; Gal. 4.6) is not Attic[15] and must be regarded as a Semitism; in all three passages in the New Testament in which ἀββά occurs (Mark 14.36; Rom. 8.15; Gal. 4.6) it is glossed as ὁ πατήρ, and in Mark 5.41 the vocative טְלִיתָא is similarly rendered τὸ κοράσιον.

Πάτερ μου (Matt. 26.39, 42) is a correct rendering of the original ἀββὰ (ὁ πατήρ) of Mark 14.36. Finally, the juxtaposition of πάτερ and ὁ πατήρ when they follow each other in the same prayer (Matt. 11.25, 26 par. Luke 10.21 beginning, end) shows that an Aramaic אַבָּא also underlies

πάτερ in Jesus' prayers. The position is very clearly illustrated by the tradition of the prayer in Gethsemane: the ἀββά used by Jesus according to Mark 14.36 is rendered ὁ πατήρ by Mark (14.36), πάτερ μου by Matthew (26.39), and πάτερ by Luke (22.42).[16]

The variation between πάτερ, ὁ πατήρ and πάτερ μου in addressing God in the Greek tradition of the prayers of Jesus can thus be explained as the result of variant translations. The reasons for them is that in the Palestinian Aramaic of the first century AD אַבָּא

was used not only as a form of address, but also for the emphatic state and for the form with the first person singular suffix, as we shall see shortly.[17] It is clear from this that the addressing of God as father goes back directly or indirectly to אַבָּא not only at Mark

14.36, where the Aramaic equivalent ἀββά is explicitly mentioned, but in the other passages as well. There can be no doubting this conclusion, as there was no other equivalent of the address 'my father' available either in Aramaic or in Hebrew, as spoken in Palestine in the time of Jesus.[18] We need not trouble ourselves in

---

[13] Blass-Debrunner-Funk, §147.3.

[14] Instances in Blass-Debrunner-Funk, *ibid.*

[15] Blass-Debrunner-Funk, *ibid.*; the nominative with the article is used in Attic only as an abrupt form of address to underlings.

[16] W. Marchel, *Abba, Père! La prière du Christ et des Chrétiens* (Analecta Biblica 19), Rome 1963, p. 138.

[17] See below, pp. 58f.

[18] See above, pp. 58f, with notes 32 and 34.

any detail over the question whether the sixteen (twenty-one, including parallels) passages[19] in which God is addressed as 'Father' in the prayers of Jesus are authentic or not beyond what has already been said on pp. 54f. The important thing is that we have discovered that all five strata of the Gospel tradition report unanimously and without any hesitation *that Jesus constantly addressed God as 'my Father'* (with the exception of Mark 15.34 par. Matt. 27.46), *and show that in so doing he used the Aramaic form* אַבָּא.

(ii) The significance of 'Abba' as an address to God

In the second part of this work we have seen that in the literature of early Palestinian Judaism there is no evidence of 'my Father' being used as a personal address to God (see above pp. 27-29). For Jesus to address God as 'my Father' is therefore something new. Whereas, for example, in the Old Testament and inter-Testamental period the traditional formula of thanksgiving 'I praise thee' is followed by the address 'Yahweh',[20] 'my Lord, my God'[21] or simply 'my Lord'[22] or '(my) God',[23] or with 'God of my father',[24] there is no precedent for Jesus' saying ἐξομολογοῦμαί σοι, πάτερ, κύριε τοῦ οὐρανοῦ καὶ τῆς γῆς (Matt. 11.25 par. Luke 10.21).

Of course, there are instances of God being addressed as πάτερ in the milieu of Hellenistic Judaism. But this is under Greek influence, and the instances are few.[25] We can say quite definitely that there is *no analogy at all* in the whole literature of Jewish prayer for God being addressed as Abba. This assertion applies not only to fixed liturgical prayer, but also to free prayer, of which many examples have been handed down to us in Talmudic literature.

We are thus confronted with a fact of the utmost significance. Whereas there is not a single instance of God being addressed as Abba in the literature of Jewish prayer, Jesus always addressed him in this way (with the exception of the cry from the cross, Mark 15.34 par.). So we have here a quite unmistakable characteristic of the *ipsissima vox Jesu*.

---

[19] They are listed above on p. 54, notes 1-5.
[20] Isa. 12.1.   [21] Ps. 86.12.
[22] 1QH 2.20, etc. Cf. G. Jeremias, *Der Lehrer der Gerechtigkeit* (SUNT 2), Göttingen 1963, p. 184, n. 13.
[23] 1QH 11.3, 15 (אֵל); Ps. Sal. 16.5 (ὁ θεός).
[24] Sirach 51.1 (Hebrew), see above, p. 28, n. 69.
[25] See above, p. 27, n. 64.

Philology reveals the reason for the striking silence of Jewish prayer literature on this point. One constantly comes across the assertion in New Testament literature that *abba*, meaning 'my father', is an emphatic state ('the father') which has secondarily taken over the function of the forms with the first person suffix ('my father', 'our father'). In reality, however, the development took place in exactly the opposite direction. The *ā* in *abbā* was not originally an appended article,[26] as in Aramaic the emphatic state is *abhā*.[27] In origin, *abba* is a pure exclamatory form, which is not inflected and which takes no possessive suffixes;[28] the gemination is modelled on the way in which a child says *imma* to its mother (the reason being that a small child says 'Mama' more often than 'Dada').[29] This form *abba*, deriving from children's speech,[30] had made considerable headway in Palestinian Aramaic in the period before the New Testament. *Abba* first suppressed the 'Imperial Aramaic'[31] and biblical-Hebraic form of address *abhi* all along the line[32]; there is, so far as I know, only one certain instance of its

[26] T. Nöldeke, Supplement to F. Schulthess-E. Littmann, *Grammatik des christlich-palästinischen Aramäisch*, Tübingen 1924, p. 156, cf. G. Schrenk, πατήρ *A,C-D, TWNT* V (1954), p. 984.24 and n. 248.

[27] E. Littmann, *Orientalia* 21 (1952), p. 389.

[28] Nöldeke, *ibid.*

[29] T. Nöldeke, 'Ausgleichungen in den semitischen Wörtern für "Vater" und "Mutter" ', in: T. Nöldeke, *Beiträge zur semitischen Sprachwissenschaft*, Strasbourg 1904, pp. 69-72, here p. 71. G. Dalman differs (*Grammatik des jüdisch-palästinischen Aramäisch²*, Leipzig 1905 = Darmstadt 1960, p. 90 and n. 1). He sees the final *ā* of *abba* as a diminutive ending which has arisen by the contraction of *ai* to a short *a* (**abbai* became *abba*); for the allegedly original **abbai* he refers to diminutive forms of proper names like Johai (from Johanan), Zakkai (from Zechariah), Mattai (from Mattaniah or Mattathiah), Abbai (from Abbaiah) (*op. cit.*, pp. 178-80, where there are many more examples).

[30] Note that in the chronological survey of the instances of *abba* as a vocative in n. 32 the two earliest examples are from children's talk.

[31] 1QGen.Ap. 2.24: יא אבי ויא מרי (the particle *ya* = oh! had until then been found only in Syriac, and not in Palestinian Aramaic).

[32] *b. Ta'an.* 23a (Bar.) ('*abba*, put me in a warm bath', Simeon b. Shatah, *c.* 90 BC), 23b ('*abba, abba*, give us rain', Hanin ha-Nehba, end of the first century BC); Gal. 4.6 (AD 49-50); Rom. 8. 15 (AD 55); '*Ed.* 5.7 ('*abba*, commend me to your colleagues', son of 'Akabiah b. Mahalalel, *c.* AD 70); Mark 14.36 (after 70); *Gen. R.* 26 on 6.1 ('*abba*, bless me' . . ., '*abba*, bless me', . . . '*abba* you have cursed me', the daughter of Gamaliel II, *c.* AD 90); *Tos. Pea* 3.8 (22.2) ('*abba*, what ails you?', undated, before 200); *Targ. Onk. Jerus. I I.* (MS Vat. Neofiti 1) Gen. 22.7; 27.18, 31, 34, 38 (*bis*); 48.18; *Targum on the Prophets, Judg.* 11.36; *Isa.* 8.4.—Palestinian Syriac: Gen. 22.7; Matt. 26.39, 42; Luke 10.21 (*bis*); 15.12, 18, 21; 16.24, 27, 30; 23.34, 46; John 11.41 12.27f.; 17.1, 5, 11, 21, 24f.

survival (apart from the mediaeval *Seder Eliyyahu Rabbah*, see above, p. 28, n. 65).[33] In addition, *abba* took over the non-vocative use of the form with the first person singular suffix[34] and replaced the emphatic state *abba*[35]; *abba* can also stand for 'his father'[36] and 'our father'.[37] Moreover, even in the pre-Christian period, *abba* is attested as a respectful address to old men.[38] This process of the extension of the use of *abba* had already come to an end in the New Testament period.[39] But despite the degree of the extension, it was never forgotten that *abba* derived from the language of small children. The Talmud says, 'When a child experiences the taste of wheat (i.e. when it is weaned) it learns to say *abba* and *imma* (i.e. these are the first sounds which it makes)'.[40] The Targum renders Isa. 8.4: 'Before the child learns to call *abba* and *imma*.' Moreover, the church fathers Chrysostom, Theodore of Mopsuestia and Theodoret of Cyrus, born in Antioch of well-to-do parents and probably growing up under the super-vision of Syrian nurses and nurserymaids, report from their own

---

[33] *Ex. R.* 46 on 34.1 (see below, n. 48).

[34] Whereas in imperial Aramaic (Dan. 5.13; 1QGen. Ap. 2.19; 6Q8 1.4) and even later in Edessene Syriac (see below, pp. 63f.), *abh(i)* was used for 'my father', in Palestinian and Babylonian Aramaic, *abba* took its place. This Aramaic *abba*, 'my father', even found its way into earlier Mishnaic Hebrew and is in fact used exclusively there, as is shown by the Mishnah and the Tosephta (see below, note 39). Here is one example out of many, *Tos. Sanh.* 9.11 (429.30f.): 'R. Eleazar b. Zadok (born *c.* AD 35) said, "When I was still a boy, I watched a priest's daughter being burnt, sitting on *abba's* shoulders." ' E. Littmann, 'Anredeformen in erweiterter Bedeutung', *NGG Phil.-hist. Klasse* 1916, pp. 94-111, has produced numerous instances of such transferences of the form of address to the other cases, which are frequent in semitic languages.

[35] This explains why the vocative *abba* repeatedly is rendered by ὁ πατήρ instead of by πάτερ (μου) in the New Testament (see the passages above, p. 55, n. 11).

[36] *Pea* 2.6; *Tos. Yoma* 1.8 (181.8).

[37] *'Er.* 6.2; *B.B.* 9.3; *Sheb.* 7.7; *Tos. Yoma* 2.5 (184.7), 6 (184.19), 8 (185.4); *Tos. B.Q.* 10.21 (368.22).

[38] See above, p. 42, n. 66.

[39] This is shown by the pre-Christian instances *b. Ta'an.* 23a (Bar.) (begin-ning of the first century BC, see above, p. 61, n. 32, *b. Ta'an.* 23b (end of the first century BC, see below, p. 58) and the New Testament (Mark 14.36; Rom. 8.15; Gal. 4.6), as well as by the fact that the authorities cited in the Mishnah and the Tosephta, including those who lived in Jerusalem before the destruction of the Temple, like R. Hanina the Captain of the Temple (*Zeb.* 9.3) and R. Eleazar b. Zadok (see above, n. 34) use *abba* without exception, and never *abhi*, when they speak of their fathers.

[40] *b. Ber.* 40a (Bar.) par. *b. Sanh.* 70b (Bar.).

experience that small children used to call their fathers *abba*.[41] But one should note that at the time of Jesus to address one's father as *abba* was no longer a practice limited to small children. The extension of the significance of *abba* which we have just outlined meant that grown up children, too, no longer addressed their father in everyday conversation as *abbi*,[42] but used *abba* instead.[43] Only when being particularly obsequious did they address their father as 'my lord',[44] like the son who was later disobedient, in the parable of the two sons (Matt. 21.29: ἐγὼ κύριε). The story of the spoilt son who is thrown out by his father because he greets a charlatan with, 'Hail, my lord, my master, my father' (קירי ברא[45] מרי אבי) is about respectful behaviour, and not about everyday language.[46] The old-fashioned *abbi* further serves to underline the obsequiousness. So we can see that to address a father as *abba* is a mark of the everyday language of the family.

As we have already pointed out, there is no instance in Jewish prayer literature of the vocative *abba* being addressed to God. But even the application of *abba* to God in the form of a statement was deliberately avoided. The Targum renders two of the three Old Testament passages in which God is called 'my father' (*abbi*) with רְבּוֹנִי (*Targ. Jer.* 3.4, 19) and only one with *abba* (*Targ. Ps.* 89.27: יקרא לי אבא את); evidently the translator felt it impossible to paraphrase the biblical text at this point. There is only one other

---

[41] T. Zahn, *Der Brief des Paulus an die Römer*[3], Leipzig-Erlangen 1925, p. 396, n. 93. The passages are: Chrysostom, *Hom. in Ep. ad Rom.* 14 on 8.15 (*PG* 60, 1862, col. 527: ὅπερ τῶν παιδίων μάλιστά ἐστι τῶν γνησίων πρὸς πατέρα ῥῆμα); Theodore of Mopsuestia, *Comm. on Rom.* 8.15 (*PG* 66, 1864, col. 824: τῶν νηπίων ἴδιόν ἐστι τὸ ἀββᾶ καλεῖν τοὺς πατέρας); Theodoret of Cyrus, *Commentary on the Pauline Epistles*, on Rom. 8.15 (*PG* 82, 1864, col. 133: τὰ γάρ τοι παιδία, πλείονι παρρησίᾳ κεχρημένα πρὸς τοὺς πατέρας — οὐδέπω γὰρ τελείαν τὴν διάκρισιν ἔχει — συχνότερον πρὸς αὐτοὺς τῇδε κέχρηται τῇ φωνῇ).

[42] Thus still 1QGen. Ap. 2.24 (see above, p. 58, n.31).

[43] '*Ed.* 5.7 (son); *Tos. Pea* 3.8 (22.2) (son); *Gen. R.* on 6.1 (*ter*) (daughter). For more on these passages see above, p. 58, n. 32.

[44] Thus a grown-up daughter: Gen. 31.35 אֲדֹנִי (compared with Judg. 11.36 אָבִי). Hellenistic Judaism: *Joseph and Aseneth* 4.3 (p. 43.21 Batiffol): κύριε; 4.6 (p. 44.3): κύριε πάτερ; 4.9 (p. 44.15): κύριέ μου πάτερ; *Test. Job* 46.2: κύριε πάτερ ἡμῶν (compare 47.1: πάτερ).

[45] Read קירי כרא (κύριε, χαῖρε), see Billerbeck II, p. 216, n. 2.

[46] *Ex. R.* 46 on 34.1.

passage in the whole of the Targum in which *abba* is applied to God (*Targ. Mal.* 2.10: הלא אבא חד לכולנא); here too, the Hebrew original made the rendering *abba* necessary. The position is exactly the same in Rabbinic literature outside the Targum. In the two passages in Tannaitic literature in which God is called אבי שבשמים,[47] *abhi*, which had virtually died out in everyday language, is used.[48] *Abba*, on the other hand, is only used of God in one passage, apart from two secondary expansions of the text.[49] This is a story which is told of Hanin ha-Nehba, a grandson of Onias the Circle-maker, famous for his prayers for rain (so called because he once drew a circle around himself and swore that he would not leave it until God gave rain).[50] As Onias was murdered in 65 BC,[51] we should put his grandson at the end of the first century BC.[52] The text reads:

Hanin ha-Nehba was the son of the daughter of Onias the Circle-maker. When the world needed rain, our teachers used to send school-children to him, who seized the hem of his coat[53] and said to him, 'Daddy, daddy, give us rain (*abba, abba*[54] *habb lan miṭra*)!' He said to Him (God): 'Master of the world, grant it (the rain) for the sake of these who are not yet able to distinguish between an *abba* who has the power to give rain and an *abba* who has not.'[55]

Abba is here used as a child's word. Hanin wants to appeal to God's mercy by using the trustful '*abba, abba*' which the school-children cry out to him in chorus and describes God in the children's language as the '*abba* who has the power to give rain'. But note that Hanin does not in any way address God himself as *abba*; his address is 'Master of the world'. So the story does not

---

[47] The two passages are cited on pp. 18 and 22.

[48] See above, p. 58. אבי occurs in secular usage only sporadically: *Tos. Sheb.* 5.6 (452.1; *v.l.* see above, p. 23, n. 47); *Ex. R.* 46 on 34.1 (see above, p. 59); a manuscript variant on *Targ. Esth. II* 1.1 (noted by G. Dalman, *The Words of Jesus*, I, ET, Edinburgh 1902, p. 192, n. 1).—Palestinian Syriac: Matt. 8.21 *v.l.* (AB).

[49] *Targ. Job* 34.36 *v.l.*; *Lev. R.* on 24.10. For these two passages see Jeremias, 'Characteristics of the *ipsissima vox Jesu*', below, pp. 109f.

[50] *Ta'an.* 3.8.   [51] Josephus, *Antt.* 14.22-24.

[52] Billerbeck IV, p. 110 ('roughly contemporaneous with Jesus'), dates Hainin ha-Nehba too late.

[53] A gesture of urgent supplication, cf. Mark 5.27.

[54] The earliest instance of *abba* as a respectful form of address (see above, p. 42, n. 66).

[55] *b. Ta'an.* 23b (cited from the Frankfurt edition, 1721). This passage was first pointed out by J. Leipoldt, *Jesu Verhältnis zu Juden und Griechen*, Leipzig 1941, pp. 136f.

affect the assertion that there is not a single instance of God being addressed as *abba* in Jewish prayers.[56]

We can see from all this why God is not addressed as *Abba* in Jewish prayers: to the Jewish mind it would have been disrespectful and therefore inconceivable to address God with this familiar word. For Jesus to venture to take this step was something new and unheard of. He spoke to God like a child to its father, simply, inwardly, confidently, Jesus' use of *abba* in addressing God reveals the heart of his relationship with God.

One often reads (and I myself believed it at one time) that when Jesus spoke to his heavenly Father he took up the chatter of a small child. To assume this would be a piece of inadmissible naivety. We have seen that even grown-up sons addressed their father as *abba*. So when Jesus addresses God as *abba* the word is by no means simply an expression of Jesus' familiarity in his converse with God. At the same time, it shows the complete surrender of the Son in obedience to the Father (Mark 14.36; Matt. 11.25f.). Indeed, the address means even more. We can see this already from the way in which Jesus never allies himself with his disciples in saying 'our Father' when he prays,[57] and distinguishes between 'my Father' and 'your Father' in what he says. This consistent distinction shows that what we established in the case of the sayings is also true of the prayers of Jesus[58]: Jesus' use of *abba* expresses a special relationship with God. It is certainly no coincidence that both in Jesus' prayer to the Father (Matt. 11.25f. par. Luke 10.21) and in his saying about the Father's action (Matt. 11.27 par. Luke 10.22) there is a recurrence of the verb ἀποκαλύπτειν, which probably was also the key word which brought the two stanzas together, and that in both sayings the content of the revelation is only hinted at in veiled language, in

[56] It is hard to understand how H. Braun, *Spätjüdisch-häretischer und frühchristlicher Radikalismus*, II (Beiträge zur historischen Theologie 24 II), Tübingen 1957, p. 127, n. 2, can assert that 'there is no essential theological difference between the Hebrew form *abbi* and the *Aramaic abba* of Jesus', in view of the clear linguistic evidence. He gives no reasons for this assertion. H. Conzelmann, 'Jesus Christus', *RGG*³ III (1959), col. 632, refers to Braun, and concludes from Rom. 8.15 that the use of the address 'abba' to God was not exclusive to Jesus. But in view of the total silence of Jewish prayer literature, Rom. 8.15 can only be understood as an echo of Jesus' prayer. How else could Paul take the cry 'Abba' to be a mark of childhood and the possession of the spirit in both Rom. 8.15 and Gal. 4.6!

[57] See above, p. 53, n. 104.   [58] See above, pp. 52-54.

each case in the same way (Matt. 11.25 par. ταῦτα, Matt. 11.27 par. πάντα). Matt. 11.27 par. makes it quite clear that in the cry of joy too, Jesus' use of *abba* expresses his certainty that he is in possession of the revelation because the Father has granted him complete divine knowledge. In Jesus' prayers too, *abba* is not only an expression of obedient trust (Mark 14.36 par.) but also at the same time a word of authority.

Only against this background can one assess the significance of Jesus' having commended the use of the address *abba* to his disciples, a fact which is demonstrated by the shorter Lucan version of the Lord's Prayer (which has been preserved in its entirety in the Matthaean version and thus must be regarded as the earlier version)[59] and confirmed by Paul (Gal. 4.6; Rom. 8.15).[60] When one considers that in the Judaism of the time of Jesus it was a characteristic of individual religious groups to have their own customs and practice of prayer[61] (we know that this is true of the Pharisees,[62] the Essenes,[63] and the disciples of John (Luke 11.1)), in other words, that the anonymous disciple who appeals to the precedent of John the Baptist (Luke 11.1) is asking Jesus for a prayer to unite and to characterize the disciples as the community of the time of salvation, and further, if one realizes that the Lord's Prayer in fact represents a brief summary of the central elements of Jesus' preaching,[64] it is possible to conclude that the giving of the Lord's Prayer to the disciples authorized them to say 'Abba', just as Jesus did. In this way, Jesus gave them a share in his relationship with God.

Jesus did not, however, stop at this authorization. At the same time he protected the new form of address to God by forbidding the disciples to use the address *abba* in everyday speech as a courtesy title (Matt. 23.9).[65] They are to reserve it for God.

The Aramaic speaking primitive church retained *abba* as a form of address to God, and the Greek-speaking communities took it

---

[59] See 'The Lord's Prayer', below, pp. 89-94.   [60] See above, p. 62, n. 56.
[61] K. H. Rengstorf, *Das Evangelium nach Lukas* (NTD 3)[9], Göttingen 1962, pp. 143f. on 11.1.
[62] See 'Daily Prayer in the Life of Jesus and the Primitive Church', below, pp. 69-72, 76f.
[63] An unedited text from Cave 4 gives the morning and evening prayers of the Essenes for each day, cf. the preliminary report by C.-H. Hunzinger, 'Aus der Arbeit an den unveröffentlichten Texten von Qumran', *TLZ* 85 (1960), cols. 151f.
[64] See 'The Lord's Prayer', below, pp. 94-107.   [65] See above, pp. 41ff.

over even outside the sphere of Pauline influence (Rom. 8.15; Gal. 4.6). While it does not appear in the Greek-speaking milieu after Mark[66]—in contrast to the survival of other alien words in liturgy like ἀμήν, ἀλληλουϊά, ὡσαννά—it remained in use in the Eastern communities, as can be seen from the ancient Syriac versions of the gospels. In Eastern Syriac, the father is addressed as אבי[67] as in imperial Aramaic,[68] and this is the word used to render the vocative πάτερ throughout the gospels by sy^cur. sin when it is not used as an address to God.[69] When, on the other hand, it is addressed to God, the Diatessaron[70] and the two witnesses of the ancient Syriac version sometimes translate it with the usual אבי[71] and sometimes with אבא, which derives from Palestinian Aramaic, but is alien to classical Syriac.[72] The fact that

---

[66] *Abba* does not seem to occur in early Christian writings in Greek and Latin outside the New Testament apart from quotations of the three New Testament passages (Gal. 4.6; Rom. 8.15; Mark 14.36). We are indebted for this observation to S. V. McCasland, 'Abba, Father', *JBL* 72 (1953), pp. 90f., who thereby contradicts his own thesis that *Abba* was such a frequent metonym for God among Jews (!) and Greek-speaking primitive Christians that it should be translated 'O God'. It only reappears later, e.g. in a prayer from the legend of Irene: Ἀββὰ ὁ πατὴρ ὁ ἀρραγὴς θεμέλιος, ὁ ἥλιος τῆς δικαιοσύνης, ἡ ἀσάλευτος πέτρα, ἡ ἄφατος δύναμις . . . (A. Wirth, *Danae in christlichen Legenden*, Vienna-Prague-Leipzig 1892, p. 127.135).

[67] The suffix *y* is written, but not spoken.   [68] See above, p. 58.

[69] Luke 15.12, 18, 21; 16.24, 27, 30 (sy^cur is defective in the last three passages).

[70] As a result of the discovery of the original Syriac text of Ephrem's Commentary on the Diatessaron, we now know how Tatian translated 'my Father', when it was addressed to God by Jesus, in at least three passages (see below, nn. 71 and 72), cf. W. Marchel, *Abba, Père!* (Analecta Biblica 19), Rome 1963, p. 140, after a communication by L. Leloir. The useful tables given by Marchel on pp. 140f. need to be corrected. Twelve instances from sy^cur should be deleted (Matt. 26.39, 42; Mark 14.36; John 11.41; 12.27f. 17.1, 5, 11, 21, 24f.), because the text of the Curetonian is not preserved in their case.

[71] Diatessaron: John 17.11. Sy^cur: Matt. 11.26; Luke 10.21b; 22.42 23.34. Sy^sin: Matt. 11.26; 26.39, 42; Mark 14.36; Luke 10.21b; John 17.1, 5 11, 21, 25.

[72] Diatessaron: Matt. 11.25; Luke 23.34. Sy^cur: Matt. 11.25; Luke 10.21a 23.46. Sy^sin: Matt. 11.26; Luke 10.21a; 11.2; 22.42; 23.46; John 11.41 12.27f.; 17.24. Sy^pesh: Matt. 11.25; Mark 14.36; Luke 22.42; 23.34; John 11.41; 12.28; 17.11, 24; Rom. 8.15; Gal. 4.6.—F. C. Burkitt, *Evangelion da-Mepharreshe*, Cambridge 1904, II, p. 47, suggests that *abba* was also the usual form for 'my father' 'in Edessene, as in most forms of Palestinian Aramaic', and that the instances in which the ancient Syriac translations of the Gospels render 'my Father' as *abba* are the last traces 'of a vanishing idiom' This hypothesis, which has no support in other classical Syriac texts (cf M. Black, *An Aramaic Approach to the Gospels and Acts*², Oxford 1954, p. 218)

the language used by Jesus has been preserved in many passages although it will have sounded strange to the ears of the Syrians of Edessa shows how established *abba* was in liturgical usage.[73]

With the simple '*Abba*, dear father', the primitive church took over the central element of Jesus' faith in God. Paul explained what the address 'Abba' meant for earliest Christianity in the Epistles to the Romans and the Galatians, tersely, but clearly; the words are different, but their content is the same. 'That[74] you are really children of God—God has sent the Spirit of his Son into our hearts, crying, "Abba! Father!"' (Gal. 4.6). 'When[75] we cry, "Abba! Father!" it is the Spirit himself bearing witness with our spirit that we are children of God' (Rom. 8.15b-16). Both remarks show how the cry of 'Abba' is beyond all human capabilities, and is only possible within the new relationship with God given by the Son (Gal.: τὸ πνεῦμα τοῦ υἱοῦ αὐτοῦ, Rom.: πνεῦμα υἱοθεσίας). It is effected by God himself through the Spirit and actualizes the divine sonship whenever it is spoken. Or, to put it more simply: whenever you cry *abba*—Paul says to his readers in each passage in the same way—God assures you that you can be absolutely certain that you really are his children. The mere fact that the communities accepted this alien word into their prayers shows how conscious they were of the new element which had been given them in the cry of 'Abba'. For them, the privilege of repeating Jesus' 'Abba' amounted to an anticipation of the fulfilment of the promise: 'I will be your father, and you will be my sons and daughters' (II Cor. 6.18 = II Sam. 7.14, free quotation).

---

stands the evidence on its head: these are not traces of an old Syriac idiom, but evidence for the infiltration of a Palestinian linguistic idiom.

[73] As it was an established Jewish custom to call prayers after their opening word, it is worth considering the old suggestion that ἀββὰ ὁ πατήρ (Rom. 8.15; Gal. 4.6) could be a reference to the beginning of the Lord's Prayer (A. Seeberg, *Der Katechismus der Urchristenheit*, Leipzig 1903 = Munich 1966, p. 243; T. Zahn, *Der Brief an die Römer*[3], Leipzig-Erlangen 1925, pp. 396f.; F. J. Dölger, *Antike und Christentum*, II, Münster 1930, pp. 152f.).

[74] Ὅτι is to be understood as declarative ('that') here, and not as a causal conjunction ('because'). Understood causally, it would make the gift of the Spirit dependent on the person being received as a child, whereas for Paul the two things go together (Rom. 8.15); furthermore, to interpret the conjunction causally would make the transition from the second person (ἐστέ) to the first (ἡμῶν) incomprehensible: 'because *you* are children of God, God has sent the Spirit of his Son into *our* hearts' is nonsense.

[75] A full stop should be put after υἱοθεσίας (v. 15b) and a comma after ὁ πατήρ (end of v. 15). To begin the sentence at v. 16 would produce a very harsh asyndeton.

II

DAILY PRAYER IN THE LIFE OF JESUS AND THE PRIMITIVE CHURCH*

I

Jesus came from a people who knew how to pray. The meaning of this statement is best understood if we consider for a moment the world surrounding Israel. At no other point does the inner corruption and decay of the Hellenistic world—especially of the Levant—in New Testament times become so apparent as in the sphere of prayer. Measured by biblical standards, Greek prayer was lacking in seriousness and reverence even in the pre-Hellenistic period. This is evident, for example, in the fact that from ancient comedy onwards, parodies of prayer had become a stock convention for comedians. Such parodies are to be found above all in Aristophanes (446-385 BC). Foolish, immoral, ridiculous, and even obscene prayers are woven into the action of the play and provoke the audience to uproarious laughter. H. Kleinknecht has devoted an entire book to this phenomenon.[1] In Hellenistic times, philosophy becomes the gravedigger of prayer. The Stoics largely disrupt belief in God. Seneca, for instance, identifies the gods and nature. Is there any sense in praying to nature? 'Why do you lift your hands towards heaven? . . . God is within you', he exclaims.[2] Like the Stoics, the Epicureans, too, assert the futility of prayer. Thus scepticism overshadows people's praying. Men pray for contradictory things. How can God hear all of them? And in that

---

* Completely revised and expanded form of a lecture delivered during the VIIIe Semaine d'Études Liturgiques at the Institut de Théologie Orthodoxe Saint-Serge, Paris, 3rd-7th July, 1961. The lecture appeared in French, 'La prière quotidienne dans la vie du Seigneur et dans l'Église primitive', in Monseigneur Cassien – B. Botte, *La prière des heures* (Lex orandi 35), Paris 1963, pp. 43-58.—I am grateful to my *Assistent*, Dr B. Schaller, for valuable references.

[1] *Die Gebetsparodie in der Antike* (Tübinger Beiträge zur Altertumswissenschaft 28), Stuttgart-Berlin 1937. [2] *To Lucilius* IV 12.1 (*Letter* 41.1)

case, what is the use of prayer? Prayer is undermined from yet another side by the mystery cults and by mysticism. Here man is deified: 'Thou art I and I am thou.'[3] The initiate, reborn, talks with God as a god. That is the death of prayer. This crisis of prayer among the educated has its effects on the people. To be sure, prayer does not cease. But men become unsure of themselves, and the infiltration of foreign religions, especially oriental cults, contributes to this uncertainty. People do not know to which deity they should pray in particular circumstances—hence the altars for the 'unknown gods', ἄγνωστοι θεοί (cf. Acts 17.23). Even if one knows to which deity to turn, one cannot be sure of a favourable hearing—how can one know for certain the right name by which the deity desires to be invoked? The thousands of magical papyri with their masses of abstruse names and epithets are moving tokens of how men had become uncertain about the efficacy of prayer. At the same time, these magical texts demonstrate something else: in a crisis about prayer, superstition grows. Prayer turns into magic everywhere. Men want to induce the deity to comply with their wishes by using mysterious names, they wear out the gods (*deos fatigare*),[4] they even threaten them. There is no more telling symptom of the decadence of the Levantine countries in early Christian times than this acute crisis into which prayer has fallen.

In Judaism all this is different, especially in the motherland, in Palestine. Here prayer maintains unshaken its position in the religious life of the people, here there is a fixed pattern for prayer, here prayer is a discipline from early youth on.

The foundation of this pattern and discipline of prayer is provided by the times fixed for daily prayer. How many of these were there? How did they originate? Neither of these questions is particularly easy to answer.

1. *The recital of the* Shᵉmaʿ *in the morning and in the evening*

The fifth book of Moses, chapter 6, contains a phrase which was regarded as the basic creed throughout the Jewish world of the time of Jesus: 'Hear, O Israel, the Lord our God is one Lord' (v. 4).[5] To this is added the divine commandment:

[3] *Papyrus Leidensis* W, 795 (ed. K. Preisendanz, *Papyri Graecae Magicae. Die griechischen Zauberpapyri*, II, Leipzig-Berlin 1931, p. 123).   [4] Cf. Matt. 6.7.
[5] The verse is thus understood as a confession of monotheism. Such was

And you shall love the Lord your God with all your heart, and with
all your soul, and with all your might. And these words which
command you this day shall be upon your heart; and you shall teach
them diligently to your children, and shall talk of them   ·

> when you sit in your house,
> and when you walk by the way,
> and when you lie down,
> and when you rise. (Deut. 6.5-7)

The last mentioned injunction to teach these words to the
children and to talk of them at every turn recurs almost identically
in Deut. 11.19. It is probably from the last words of this injunction, 'when you lie down and when you rise', that the custom of
beginning and ending each day with the confession of the one
God derives. It became a general Jewish practice in pre-Christian
times. 'Twice a day, at its beginning and when the hour of sleep
approaches, it is fitting to remember in gratitude before God the
gifts which he gave (us) after the deliverance from Egypt', remarks Josephus in the *Jewish Antiquities*.[6] The custom of reciting
the creed in the morning between dawn and sunrise[7] and in the
evening after sunset[8] is first attested in the second century BC by
the *Letter of Aristeas* (145-100 BC).[9] It was observed in Palestine[10]
as well as in the Diaspora.[11] The Essenes[12] and the Therapeutae,[13]
too, had prayers at sunrise and in the evening. The texts recited
were the creed of Deut. 6.4 followed by the subsequent verses 5-9

---

the interpretation given to it by the Septuagint and earlier Rabbinic exegesis
(R. Eleazar b. Azariah, *c.* AD 100, b. Ḥag. 3a). Earlier exegesis thus stressed
that there is no other God than Yahweh. Only after AD 300 is an alternative
interpretation of the text put forward by many scholars: 'The Lord is our
God, the Lord alone.' This stresses that Yahweh, and no other God, is the
God of Israel. cf. Billerbeck II, pp. 28-30.

[6] *Antt.* 4.212.

[7] Wisdom 16.28: 'We must rise before the sun to give thee thanks.'

[8] *Ber.* 1.1: from sunset to ten o'clock in the evening (Rabbi Eliezer, *c.* AD
90, representing the older tradition).

[9] 160. The morning prayer is also mentioned by itself at 304f.

[10] Billerbeck IV, pp. 189-207.

[11] *Pseudo-Aristeas* 160; Philo, *De spec. leg.* 4.141. For morning prayer alone
cf. Ps.-Aristeas 304f. (see n. 9); Wisdom 16.28; *Sib. Or.* 3.591f.

[12] 1QS 10. 1-3, 9, 11, 13f.; 1QH 12.4-7. An unpublished papyrus manuscript from Cave 4 (*c.* 100-50 BC) contains the benedictions of the morning
and evening prayers for each day of the month (C.-H. Hunzinger, 'Aus der
Arbeit an den unveröffentlichten Texten von Qumran', *TLZ* 85, 1960,
col. 152).   [13] Philo, *De vita contempl.* 27.

hen came Deut. 11.13-21, because the clause 'when you lie down
nd when you rise' (6.7: see above) recurs in 11.19; as a conclu-
ion, there was Num. 15.41, a solemn self-declaration of God.[14]
The creed, called *Sh^ema^*, 'Hear', after the opening words of Deut.
.4, 'Hear, O Israel', had benedictions before it and after it. All
men, and boys from their twelfth birthday upwards, had to recite
he *Sh^ema^* regularly, whereas women, children and slaves were
ree from this obligation (as well as from all others that had to be
erformed at specific times, because their time was not at their
wn disposal).[15] Boys were taught the words as soon as they could
peak.[16] To recite the *Sh^ema^* twice a day was considered the
ninimum of religious practice. Evading this custom meant
eparating oneself from the religious community. R. Eliezer b.
Iyrcanus (*c.* AD 90) said: 'Who is an עַם הָאָרֶץ (i.e. an unreligious
rute)? He who does not recite the *Sh^ema^* in the morning and in
he evening.'[17]

2. *The three hours of prayer*

Curiously enough, we find an analogous yet quite different
ustom alongside the twofold recitation of the *Sh^ema^*: the custom
f praying *three* times a day. It is first attested in the book of
Daniel, 6.11 (cf. also v.14), that is in the year 164 BC. Here it is said
hat Daniel had windows in his upper room which opened in the
irection of Jerusalem and that he used to kneel down three times
 day, to pray, and to praise God.[18] Of these three hours of prayer
—morning, afternoon and evening[19]—the first to be attested
ndividually is the afternoon prayer, which was made at 3 p.m.,
hen the daily afternoon sacrifice was offered in the Temple. The
ook of Ezra, which took its present form towards the end of the
hird century BC, already says that Ezra uttered his great peni-
ential prayer 'at the evening sacrifice' (9.5). Daniel, too, made his
enitential prayer 'at the time of the evening sacrifice' (9.21). The

[14] Num. 15.41 is an ancient element of the *Sh^ema^*, as is borne out by
osephus, *Antt.* 4.212. By contrast, Num. 15.37-40 is presumably a later
ddition (I. Elbogen, *Studien zur Geschichte des jüdischen Gottesdienstes*, Schriften
r Lehranstalt für die Wissenschaft des Judentums 1, Berlin 1907, pp. 17f.;
, *Der jüdische Gottesdienst in seiner geschichtlichen Entwicklung*[3], Frankfurt-M.
931 = [4]Hildesheim 1962, pp. 24f.).

[15] *Ber.* 3.3. [16] *b. Sukka* 42a (Bar.). [17] *b. Ber.* 47b (Bar.).

[18] It is doubtful whether the three fixed times are already presupposed by
s. 55.17, where the suppliant says: 'Evening and morning and at noon I
ter my complaint and moan, and he will hear my voice.' [19] *Ber.* 4.1.

same time is mentioned for Judith's prayer (9.1, c. 150 BC). Thi
means that while in the Holy City the crowds gathered in th
Temple to be present at the offering of the afternoon sacrific
(Acts 3.1), people outside Jerusalem united in prayer with th
community assembled in the Temple. We shall return later to thi
connection of the afternoon prayer with the Temple cult.

One might conclude from all this that the three hours of praye
came about through the addition of the afternoon prayer to th
morning and the evening *Sh*ᵉ*ma*ᶜ.[20] However, such a conclusio
cannot be sustained. The prayer said at the three fixed hours is of
completely different character from the *Sh*ᵉ*ma*ᶜ. The latter is not
prayer at all, but a creed, surrounded by benedictions. As a matte
of fact, Rabbinic literature never speaks of 'praying the *Sh*ᵉ*ma*ᶜ'
but always of 'reciting the *Sh*ᵉ*ma*ᶜ' (קְרִיאַת שְׁמַע).[21] By contras
the three hours of prayer were strictly devoted to prayer. Th
prayer used on these occasions was the *T*ᵉ*philla*, i.e. 'The Prayer
the Grand Benediction. The *T*ᵉ*philla* is a hymn consisting of
string of benedictions. At the end of the first century AD the
number was fixed at eighteen, and consequently the *T*ᵉ*philla* wa
also called the 'Eighteen Benedictions'.[22] To these, the person wh
prayed added his or her private petitions.[23] There is a furthe
indication of the difference in character between the *Sh*ᵉ*ma*ᶜ an
the *T*ᵉ*philla*: as mentioned above, only free men were obliged t
recite the *Sh*ᵉ*ma*ᶜ, whereas the *T*ᵉ*philla* was to be said by al
including women, children, and even slaves.

As a matter of fact, the custom of praying three times a day ha
quite a different origin from the twofold recital of the *Sh*ᵉ*ma*
We have already seen from various pieces of evidence that th
afternoon prayer was said at the time of the afternoon sacrific
In all probability, there must therefore be a connection betwee
this prayer and the institution of the so-called 'standing post
(Hebrew מַעֲמָדוֹת). In order to understand this, one has
remember a basic fact about the organization of the Jerusale
Temple cult. Apart from a number of superior priests and officia
the rank and file of priests and levites who served in the Temp
were not permanently in residence. Neither priests nor levites we

---

[20] I myself expounded this view in the lecture mentioned above, p. 66, n.
[21] Billerbeck IV, p. 189.
[22] Billerbeck IV, pp. 208-49.   [23] Billerbeck IV, pp. 233f.

members of a profession, but were hereditary classes into which a man was born, whose members lived scattered all over Palestine. After the exile, they had been organized into twenty-four courses (מִשְׁמָרוֹת), each of which in turn had to go up to Jerusalem for a week of service. Each of these courses had a lay group called a 'standing post' (מַעֲמָד). Part of it accompanied the priests and Levites to Jerusalem and was present during the sacrifice as representatives of the people (שְׁלוּחִין). The other part remained at home, and during its priestly course's week of service assembled in the synagogue to read the scriptures and pray, thus participating in the Temple service from a distance. These men would gather three times a day: in the morning at the time of the morning burnt offering, in the afternoon at three o'clock when the afternoon sacrifice was burnt, and in the evening at sunset 'when the Temple gates were closed (נְעִילָה)'.[24] There can be no doubt that it was above all the members of the Pharisaic groups who volunteered to serve in the מַעֲמָדוֹת and to pray in lieu of the people of their district. Presumably the Pharisees, too, were responsible for extending the prayers said daily by the 'standing posts' during their week of service over the whole year.[25] They probably also extended the obligation of saying the Tephilla to all members of a household, including women, children and slaves.[26]

The *Psalms of Solomon*, which were composed about 50 BC in Pharisaic circles, contain a moving appeal to take this duty seriously and to praise God 'at his awakening':

Why sleepest thou, O my soul,
   and blessest not the Lord?
Sing a new song,
   unto God who is worthy to be praised.
Sing and be wakeful at his awakening. (Ps. Sal. 3.1f., Charles II, pp. 634f.)

[24] *Ta'an.* 4.4. The rabbi quoted as an authority in the discussion, R. Joshua Hananiah, had himself served as a Levitic singer in the Temple (*b.* '*Arak.* 11b (*Bar.*); *Siphre Num.* 116 on 18.3).
[25] This is suggested by the fact that the book of Judith, which knows the three hours of prayer (morning prayer: 12.5f.; prayer at the time of the afternoon sacrifice: 9.1; evening prayer: 13.3), is of Pharisaic origin. Further evidence is provided by Matt. 6.5f.: the prayer in public to which Jesus takes exception occurs at one of the three fixed hours, and all of Matt. 6.1-18 is antipharisaic.
[26] *Ber.* 3.3.

Psalm 6.4f. tells how the father of a family intercedes in his morning prayer for all his house:

He ariseth from his sleep and blesseth the name of the Lord:
  When his heart is at peace, he singeth to the name of his God,
And he entreateth the Lord for all his house. (Ps. Sal. 6.4f., Charles II, p. 639)

By New Testament times, the custom of praying three times a day seems to have become a general rule, to judge from Acts 3.1; 10.3, 30; Didache 8.3. The two customs of reciting the *Sh*ᵉ*ma*ᶜ twice a day and praying three times a day were fused in the following manner: In the morning, the pious Jew would combine the *T*ᵉ*philla* with the *Sh*ᵉ*ma*ᶜ.[27] In the afternoon he would pray only the *T*ᵉ*philla* (this hour was called 'the hour of the Prayer' Acts 3.1). In the evening, he would again recite the *Sh*ᵉ*ma*ᶜ and pray the *T*ᵉ*philla*. Of all these obligations, only the evening prayer seems to have met with some opposition. At the end of the first century AD scholars still debated whether it was a general obligation to pray the *T*ᵉ*philla* in the evening in addition to the *Sh*ᵉ*ma*ᶜ,[28] but practice had long defeated theory on this point.[29]

Thus we see that sunrise, afternoon (3 p.m.) and sunset were the three daily times of prayer for the Jews of the New Testament era. In the morning and in the evening, they would recite the *Sh*ᵉ*ma*ᶜ framed by benedictions and followed by the *T*ᵉ*philla*; in the afternoon the latter was prayed alone. These three hours of prayer together with the benedictions said before and after meals, were Israel's great treasure, the skeleton framework for an education in prayer and for the practice of prayer for everyone from their youth upwards.

II

About the *prayer of Jesus* we know little. If we search the Synoptic Gospels, we encounter only two prayers of Jesus—apart from the three exclamatory prayers in the crucifixion narrative. These two prayers are the cry of jubilation (Matt. 11.25f. par.) and the prayer in Gethsemane (Mark 14.36 par.). The Gospel of John adds three

---

[27] Billerbeck II, pp. 700f.
[28] Billerbeck II, pp. 151, 697; IV, pp. 220f. The rabbis found it hard to find proof from scripture for the evening *T*ᵉ*philla* (*j. Ber.* 4.7b.3).
[29] Billerbeck IV, p. 220.

more: the short prayer in the story of Lazarus (11.41f.), the equally short prayer in the Temple forecourt (the Johannine Gethsemane prayer 12.27f.), and the High Priestly prayer (17), of which at least the last is coloured to a high degree by the language and style of the evangelist. This is little enough material. We can add a number of general references to the praying of Jesus, especially to his prayers in solitude (Mark 1.35; 6.46 par. Matt. 14.23, and above all in Luke: 3.21; 5.16; 6.12; 9.18, 28f.),[30] a saying of Jesus about his prayer for Peter (Luke 22.31f.) and finally his instructions to the disciples on prayer, which are dominated by the Lord's Prayer. How we would like to know more!

Actually we do know more! We know that Jesus was brought up in a devout home (Luke 2, cf. 4.16); we know therefore that he participated in the liturgical heritage of his people, and consequently we know the prayers which the child Jesus was taught in his parental home and which accompanied the man Jesus throughout his life. The three hours of prayer in particular were so universally observed among the Jews of Jesus' time that we are justified in including them in the comment 'as his custom was', which is made in Luke with reference to Jesus' attendance at Sabbath worship (Luke 4.16).

But we are not limited to this conclusion alone; particular references are not lacking. In Mark 1.35 we find Jesus at prayer before sunrise ('in the early morning, a great while before day'). After the Feeding of the Five Thousand, Jesus ascends a mountain in the evening to pray (Mark 6.46), and when Luke relates that Jesus continued all night in prayer before the choosing of the twelve apostles (ἦ διανυκτερεύων ἐν τῇ προσευχῇ τοῦ θεοῦ, Luke 6.12), this is evidently the evening prayer which he has extended till dawn. Luke 10.26 should also be mentioned in connection with the daily morning and evening prayer of Jesus. When Jesus asks the scribe πῶς ἀναγινώσκεις; here, and the scribe answers with the commandment from the *Sh^ema*' to love God (Deut. 6.5), the question does not (or, originally did not) mean 'How do you read?', for ἀναγινώσκειν here represents קרא, meaning 'to recite'. With his question 'How do you recite?', Jesus takes it for granted that the daily recital of the creed is a common practice. There is confirmation of this in the report in Mark 12.29f. that Jesus answered the question about the greatest commandment not only

[30] On the Lucan passages see below, p. 76.

with the commandment to love God (Deut. 6.5), but in addition, with the preceding verse as well: 'Hear, O Israel, the Lord our God is one Lord . . .', so accustomed is he to reciting the *Sh^ema'*.

Two passages show that Jesus was also accustomed to the other time of prayer, the third, in the afternoon. Luke 18.9-14 describes two men who went up into the Temple to pray, no doubt at the regular 'hour of prayer', at 3 p.m. (Acts 3.1). The allusion to the afternoon prayer is even clearer in Matt. 6.5, where Jesus rebukes the hypocrites who pray publicly on the street corner. This can hardly mean that the Pharisees regularly posted themselves in the market-place to pray. We have rather to remember that at the moment in the afternoon sacrifice when the whole congregation prayed, loud trumpets were sounded from the Temple over the city of Jerusalem (Sirach 50.16; *Tam.* 7.3) to mark the hour of prayer for its inhabitants. So what happens is that the Pharisees whom Jesus rebukes contrive—apparently quite unintentionally and by chance—to be at that moment in the midst of the crowds, and so to be obliged to pray in public. There is one indirect piece of evidence for supposing that Jesus not only knew but also himself observed this afternoon prayer. The first benediction of the *T^ephilla*—this benediction dates from before the destruction of the Temple in AD 70[31]—contains two strikingly solemn invocations of God. What is presumably the oldest form of this benediction runs as follows[32]:

> Blessed be thou, Lord (our God and the God of our fathers),
>> the God of Abraham, the God of Isaac and the God of Jacob
>>> (God great, mighty and fearful),
>> most high God,
>> master[33] of heaven and earth,
>> our shield and the shield of our fathers (our trust in every generation).
> Blessed be thou, Lord, the shield of Abraham.

[31] Billerbeck I, pp. 406f.

[32] Billerbeck IV, p. 211, following the text of Dalman, *Die Worte Jesu*, I[1], Leipzig 1898, p. 299; Palestinian recension, later additions in brackets.

[33] The invocation קונה שמים וארץ is taken from Gen. 14.19, 22. In that passage, קנה does not mean 'to acquire, possess', as usually in the O.T., but 'to create' (as in Deut. 32.6; Ps. 139.13; probably there were originally two independent roots). Ancient Judaism in practice ignored this sense so that the invocation was taken to mean 'Master of heaven and earth' (cf. 1QGen.Ap. 22.16, 21 אל עליון מרה שמיא וארעא; *Targ. Onk. Gen.* 14.19, 22 אל עילאה דקנינה שמיא וארעא; so too Matt. 11.25 par. κύριε τοῦ οὐρανοῦ καὶ τῆς γῆς).

When Jesus speaks of God as the God of Abraham and the God of Isaac and the God of Jacob (Mark 12.26 par.) and when he, ordinarily so sparing in the use of divine names, calls God 'Lord of heaven and earth' in Matt. 11.25, this twofold coincidence with the wording of the first benediction of the *T^ephilla* indicates Jesus' familiarity with it. This conclusion is enforced not only by the fact that each of these two invocations of God occurs only in one pericope in the Old Testament (Ex. 3.6, 15, 16 and Gen. 14.19, 22), but also by the fact that they are not in use in Palestinian Judaism outside the *T^ephilla*. Moreover, as we shall see shortly, these three times of prayer were firmly established in the primitive church; the observance of afternoon prayer in particular is attested in Acts 3.1. It is highly improbable that the early church would have kept the hours of prayer if Jesus had rejected them.

So we may conclude with all probability that no day in the life of Jesus passed without the three times of prayer: the morning prayer at sunrise, the afternoon prayer at the time when the afternoon sacrifice was offered in the Temple, the evening prayer at night before going to sleep. We can sense from this something of the hidden inner life of Jesus, something of the source from which he daily drew strength.

Only when we have appreciated the position of Jesus within the liturgical tradition and the way in which the three times of prayer were a daily habit with him can we see the other side as well, the extent to which Jesus' prayer shatters custom.

The first thing to be noticed is that Jesus is not content with the pious practice of liturgical prayer three times a day. The most important passages are:

Mark 1.35: 'And in the morning, rising up a great while before day, he went out, and departed into a solitary place.'

Simon and those with him notice Jesus' absence, and prepare to look for him, so long is he gone.

Mark 6.46: 'And when he had sent them away he departed into a mountain to pray.'

Again it must have been a long prayer in solitude; it is only about the fourth watch of the night (3-6 a.m.) that the disciples catch sight of him (v. 48).

Luke 6.12: 'He went up into a mountain to pray, and continued all night in prayer to God.'

Now it is very probable that parts of the passages in the gospels which mention Jesus' prayer are to be attributed to the editing of the evangelists. Thus Luke repeatedly adds the motif of the praying Lord to the text of Mark (5.16; 6.12; 9.18, 28; cf. 3.21). But even so, the question remains: what induced Luke to add this motif to the Marcan text? The most likely answer is the existence of a firmly established tradition about Jesus' prayer in solitude by night. This answer, moreover, commends itself to us because we do in fact have an old tradition describing how Jesus, outside the regular time of prayer, invokes his Father in the middle of the night: Gethsemane (Mark 14.32-42 par.).

Another feature shows how far Jesus departs from custom. The *Shema'* and the *Tephilla* are Hebrew prayers.[34] It is true that the *Kaddish* which served to round off the synagogue service is in Aramaic, but this is an exception due to the fact that the *Kaddish* is the prayer with which the preacher ended his sermon, which was delivered in Aramaic. In contrast with the *Shema'* and the *Tephilla*, the Lord's Prayer is an Aramaic prayer. This is shown by the words ὀφείλημα / ὀφείλειν which are typical Aramaisms, and by the way in which the first two petitions directly echo the *Kaddish*.[35] Moreover, the invocation of God as 'Abba',[36] coined by Jesus, is also Aramaic, as is finally the cry from the cross (Mark 15.34). Thus Jesus not only prayed in his native tongue in his private prayers, he also gave his disciples a formal prayer couched in the vernacular when he taught them the Lord's Prayer. In so doing, he removes prayer from the liturgical sphere of sacred language and places it right in the midst of everyday life.

Jesus' prayer breaks the confines of religious custom not only in the times and in the language of prayer, but above all in its content. Let us start with Luke 11.1. According to this passage, the occasion for teaching the Lord's Prayer was the request of one

---

[34] Theoretically, both the *Shema'* (Billerbeck IV, p. 196) and the *Tephilla* (Billerbeck IV, p. 220) might be said in any language. But it is hardly an accident that both texts have come down to us only in Hebrew, not in Aramaic. Moreover, the benedictions to be said before and after the *Shema'* are Hebrew, as are also the Essene benedictions to be said in the morning and in the evening (see above, n. 12).

[35] Cf. 'The Lord's Prayer' below, pp. 98ff.

[36] See above, pp. 54-65.

of the disciples: 'Lord, teach us to pray, as John taught his disciples.' What is meant by this 'teach us to pray'? Surely not that the anonymous disciple wanted to assert that the twelve had never learned how to pray and had first to be taught how to do it. Rather, one needs to remember that religious groups were distinguished among other things by their characteristic prayers.[37] We know this of the Pharisees (as we have seen, the custom of the three daily times of prayer is probably originally Pharisaic); we can now observe it with the Essenes[38]; and we learn from Luke 11.1 that the disciples of John had their own prayers, too. So we must conclude that the disciples asked for a prayer to be a characteristic of Jesus' followers, i.e. to be a distinguishing formula to be used either in addition to the traditional prayers or actually as a substitute for them. At any rate, as we shall see shortly, the Church regarded the Lord's Prayer as a substitute for the three daily Jewish prayers long before the gospels were composed. As we know from Didache 9-10, the Church also had its own grace before and after meals, and in so doing probably follows the example of Jesus. From all this, it follows that in Luke 11.1 Jesus is asked for a fixed prayer which will correspond to his message. 'Teach us to pray as men should pray who are already partakers of the coming reign of God.' The Lord's Prayer is in fact a brief summary of the fundamentals of Jesus' proclamation, with the address 'Father', the prayer for the final redemption (the two petitions in the second person), the prayer for the present realization—here and now—of the saving gifts of God (the two petitions in the third person), and the last petition for preservation from apostasy in the last terrible hour of temptation.

But if Jesus gave his disciples a new prayer of their own, it may be supposed that he himself was not content with the liturgically prescribed texts, the *Sh*e*ma*ʿ and the *T*e*philla*. The tradition that Jesus prayed alone for long hours and through whole nights is in itself evidence of this. And there is a further consideration to support the suggestion. All the prayers of Jesus in all four gospels have this in common, that except for the cry on the cross אלי אלי למה שבקתני, where the invocation is taken from Ps. 22.1,[39]

---

[37] K. H. Rengstorf, *Das Evangelium nach Lukas* (NTD 3)⁹, Göttingen 1962, pp. 143f. ad loc.

[38] See above, n. 12.

[39] For the wording, cf. J. Jeremias, 'Das Gebetsleben Jesu', *ZNW* 25 (1926), pp. 123-40, here p. 130, n. 8.

they all invoke God as 'Father'.[40] From a comparison of Mark 14.36 with Rom. 8.15; Gal. 4.6 on the one hand, and from the variation between πάτερ, πάτερ μου, ὁ πατήρ which are alternative translations, on the other hand, we can conclude that Jesus always used the word אבא. This Aramaic 'Abba', which is a colloquialism originally stemming from the language of children, is nowhere attested in Jewish prayers. It definitely represents Jesus' own most characteristic mode of speech and it is the profoundest expression of his authority and of his consciousness of his mission (Matt. 11.27). It is hardly conceivable that this 'Abba' could have been absent from his daily prayers during the three hours of prayer.

A new way of praying is born. Jesus talks to his Father as naturally, as intimately and with the same sense of security as a child talks to his father. It is a characteristic token of this new mode of prayer that it is dominated by thanksgiving. The only personal prayer of Jesus of some length from the time before the passion is a thanksgiving in spite of failure (Matt. 11.25 par. Luke 10.21). An echo of this predominance of thanksgiving is preserved in John 11.41, where Jesus gives thanks *before* being heard. There is a profound reason for this predominance of thanksgiving in Jesus' prayer. A fine saying from Tannaitic times[41] runs[42]:

> In the world to come all sacrifices will cease, but the thank-offering will remain for ever; likewise all confessions will cease, but the confession of thanks will remain for ever.

Thanksgiving is one of the foremost characteristics of the new age. So when Jesus gives thanks he is not just following custom. There is more to it than that; he is actualizing God's reign here and now.

III

The picture which emerges from our examination of the gospels is repeated when we turn to the *early church*. Here too, as in con-

---

[40] For a full treatment see 'Abba', above, pp. 54-65.
[41] 1st-2nd century AD.
[42] *Pesik.* 79a.17-19 (ed. S. Buber, Lyck 1868).

temporary Judaism and as in the life of Jesus, we find the three hours of prayer to be a firmly established practice. Didache 8.3, which says, referring to the Lord's Prayer, 'Three times a day you shall pray thus', is particularly important. The Acts of the Apostles twice refers to the afternoon prayer at 3 p.m. (Acts 3.1; 10.3, 30). Paul also should be mentioned here. When he says that he prays 'continually', 'without ceasing', 'always', 'day and night', we are not to think of uninterrupted praying but of his observance of the regular hours of prayer. The phrase 'to be instant in prayer' (προσκαρτερεῖν τῇ προσευχῇ Rom. 12.12; Col. 4.2) is to be understood in a similar way, for προσκαρτερεῖν here means 'faithfully to observe a rite' (as in Acts 1.14; 2.46; 6.4).

But the early church, too, is not content with liturgical custom. Peter prays at twelve noon (Acts 10.9), outside the regular time, and the Jerusalem Church prays at night for the imprisoned Apostle (12.5, 12); Paul and Silas praise God in prison at midnight (16.25). Vigils, i.e. the extension of evening prayer far into the night, even right through the night, are often held, as is shown by the passages in which Paul talks of his ἀγρυπνίαι, his vigils (II Cor. 6.5; 11.27). In Eph. 6.18 the readers are summoned to ἀγρυπνεῖν in prayer (cf. Luke 21.36 ἀγρυπνεῖτε δὲ ἐν παντὶ καιρῷ δεόμενοι ἵνα . . .). The nocturnal Passover celebration of the Quartodecimans, during which prayers were offered for Israel in expectation of the parousia of the Kyrios at midnight, shows that the Easter vigil, i.e. the service of intercession for Israel during the night of the 14th-15th Nisan, dates back to very early times.[43]

Like Jesus, the early church breaks through the bonds of ancient Jewish custom not only in the case of the fixed times of prayer but also in the prayers which were said at them. We can see this from the way in which Deut. 6.5, 'You shall love the Lord your God with all your heart, and with all your soul, and with all your might', is quoted in the first three gospels (Mark 12.30, 33; Matt. 22.37; Luke 10.27).[44] These quotations present an exceedingly striking, even enigmatic, picture. A table may make this clear:

[43] Cf. J. Jeremias, *The Eucharistic Words of Jesus*, ET², London 1966, pp. 122-5, 212-14.
[44] For what follows, see J. Jeremias, 'Die Muttersprache des Evangelisten Matthäus', *ZNW* 50 (1959), 270-4 (*Abba*, Göttingen 1966, pp. 255-60).

Deut. 6.5	Deut. 6.5 LXX	Mark 12.30	Mark 12.33	Matt. 22.37	Luke 10.27
heart	heart (Brescr. mind)	heart	heart	heart	heart
soul	soul	soul mind	understanding	soul mind	soul
strength	might (Ἄλλος: strength)	strength	strength		strength
					mind

The first thing to be noted is that all four of these quotations deviate from the Old Testament text. In the second place, it must be observed that they also deviate from each other, in Mark even within one and the same pericope. In Mark 12.30 and Luke 10.27, the tripartite form has given way to a four part one which may well have arisen from the insertion of 'mind' as an alternative translation for לֵבָב 'heart', which stands first in the Massoretic text. In Mark, however, it occupies the third place, whereas Luke has it in the fourth. In Mark 12.33 and Matt. 22.37, on the other hand, the tripartite structure of the saying is preserved, but the wording differs from the Old Testament text. In Mark 12.33, 'soul' is represented by 'understanding', whereas the parallels, including the Septuagint, read 'soul'. In Matt. 22.37, 'mind' occupies third position and 'strength' is omitted (no doubt this is an abbreviation of Mark 12.30).

These divergences of the four quotations both from the biblical text and from each other are puzzling, because we have to do not with a random saying but with an important liturgical text, in fact with the most important text in all Jewish literature, the beginning of the creed which was recited twice every day. Curiously enough, the problem which is raised here has not even been noticed by the commentaries. As far as I am aware, the only one to have drawn attention to it was T. W. Manson, and he was courageous enough to confess that, 'Mk. XII. 29f. (Deut. VI. 4f.) presents a very complex textual problem, which I am unable to solve'.[45]

In my opinion, there is no other explanation for this phenomenon than that the Greek *Shᵉma'* was not a regularly recited liturgical text for any of the three synoptic evangelists. At least at the

[45] 'The Old Testament in the Teaching of Jesus', *BJRL* 34 (1951-2), pp. 312-32, here p. 318.

time of the composition of the synoptic gospels, that is to say after the fall of Jerusalem, the *Sh^ema'* was no longer recited three times daily in the Greek-speaking church.

What prayers then *did* the church say at the three appointed times each day? The answer to this question comes from the instructions about the Lord's Prayer which are given in the Didache, 8.3 (see above): 'Three times daily you shall pray thus.' The prayer said at the three hours of prayer was the Lord's Prayer.

The extent to which the informal prayers spoken on these occasions were also filled with a totally new meaning is shown by Paul's remarks about the μνεία, the regular prayer of intercession (e.g. I Thess. 1.2; Phil. 1.3-6; Rom. 1.9f.). Paul did not confine this to his own communities, but also included churches not founded by him, such as the church of Rome (Rom. 1.9f.) and the church of Colossae (Col. 1.9, cf 2.1-3).

To sum up: both the prayers of Jesus and those of the early church stand in the liturgical tradition. The custom of praying three times a day is taken over from Judaism, but the new life bestowed through the gospel shatters the fixed liturgical forms, especially with regard to the content of prayers.

What is new here can be summed up in one word, 'Abba'.

III

THE LORD'S PRAYER IN THE LIGHT
OF RECENT RESEARCH

1. THE LORD'S PRAYER IN THE ANCIENT CHURCH[1]

DURING the time of Lent and Easter in the year AD 350, a Jerusalem presbyter, Cyril by name, who was consecrated as bishop a year later, presented his celebrated twenty-four Catechetical Lectures in the Church of the Holy Sepulchre. These lectures, which have been preserved for us through the shorthand notes of one of Cyril's hearers,[2] fall into two parts. Those in the first part prepared the candidates for the baptism which they were to receive on Easter Eve. The focal point of these prebaptismal lectures was the exposition of the confession of faith, the Jerusalem Creed. The last five lectures, however, were presented during Easter week. These postbaptismal lectures instructed the newly baptized about the sacraments which they had received. For this reason they were called 'mystagogical catechetical lectures', that is, lectures which introduced the hearers to the 'mysteries' or sacraments of the Christian faith. In the last of these mystagogical lectures, Cyril explains for his hearers the liturgy of the Mass, or Service of Holy Communion, especially the prayers which are spoken there. Among these is the Lord's Prayer.

This final (twenty-fourth) Catechetical Lecture by Cyril of Jerusalem is our earliest proof for the fact that the Lord's Prayer was regularly employed in the Service. The position in the Service where the Lord's Prayer was prayed is to be noted: it came

[1] See P. Fiebig, *Das Vaterunser*, Gütersloh 1927; E. Lohmeyer, *The Lord's Prayer*, *ET*, London 1965 (however, Lohmeyer's observations on the Aramaic original of the Lord's Prayer are untenable); T. W. Manson, 'The Lord's Prayer', *BJRL* 38 (1955-6), pp. 99-113, 436-48; H. Schürmann, *Das Gebet des Herrn*, Leipzig 1957.

[2] The Greek text and an English translation are conveniently given in F. L. Cross ed., *St Cyril of Jerusalem's Lectures on the Christian Sacraments* (Texts for Students 51), London 1951, or, translation alone, in W. Telfer ed., *Cyril of Jerusalem and Nemesius of Emesa* (The Library of Christian Classics IV), Philadelphia, Pennsylvania, 1955.

immediately before the Communion. As a constituent part of the Communion liturgy, the Lord's Prayer belonged to that portion of the Service in which only those who were baptized were permitted to participate, i.e., it belonged to the so-called *missa fidelium* or 'Service for the baptized'. The late Professor T. W. Manson[3] has shown that this leads to the conclusion that knowledge of the Lord's Prayer and the privilege to use it were reserved for the full members of the church.

What we have demonstrated for Jerusalem holds for the ancient church as a whole. Everywhere the Lord's Prayer was a constituent part of the celebration of the Lord's Supper, and everywhere the Lord's Prayer, together with the creed, belonged to those items in which the candidates for baptism were instructed either just before baptism or, as we saw in the case of Cyril, in the days directly after baptism. Petition by petition, the Lord's Prayer was elucidated, and then the whole recapitulated in an address to the converts. Thus those seeking baptism or those newly baptized learned the Lord's Prayer by heart. They were allowed to join in praying it for the first time in their first Service of Holy Communion, which was attached to the rite of their baptism. Henceforth they prayed it daily, and it formed a token of their identification as Christians. Because the privilege of praying the Lord's Prayer was limited to the baptized members of the church, it was called the 'prayer of believers'.

The connection of the Lord's Prayer with baptism can be traced back to early times. In the beginning of the second century, we find a variant to Luke 11.2 which reads: 'Thy Holy Spirit come upon us and cleanse us.' The heretic Marcion (about AD 140) had this instead of the first petition. His wording of the Lord's Prayer seems to have been as follows: 'Father, Thy Holy Spirit come upon us and cleanse us. Thy kingdom come. Thy bread for the morrow give us day by day. And forgive us our sins, for we also forgive everyone who is indebted to us. And do not allow us to be led into temptation.' Two of the Greek minuscule manuscripts (numbers 162, 700) and two late church fathers (Gregory of Nyssa †394, and Maximus Confessor †662) have the petition for the Holy Spirit instead of the second petition. It is quite improbable that the petition for the Holy Spirit should be the original text; its attestation is much too weak. From where, then, does this petition

[3] 'The Lord's Prayer', pp. 99-113, 436-48.

originate? We know that it was an old baptismal prayer, and we may conclude that it was added to the Lord's Prayer when this was used at the baptismal ceremony. One may compare the fact that the Marcionite version of the Prayer, quoted above, has, in the petition for bread, 'Thy bread'. This is probably an allusion to the Lord's Supper; thus Marcion has both sacraments in view, baptism in this first petition and the Lord's Supper, which followed baptism, in his phrase 'Thy bread'.

But we must go even one step further back. The connection of the Lord's Prayer with baptism which we have found already in the first part of the second century can be traced back even into the first century. It is true that at first glance, we seem to get a completely different picture when we turn to the *Didache*, or *Teaching of the Twelve Apostles*. This document is the oldest 'church order', the basic part of which is dated by its most recent commentator, perhaps somewhat too optimistically, as early as AD 50-70,[4] but which in all likelihood does nonetheless belong in the first Christian century. In the *Didache* (8.2), the Lord's Prayer is cited, word for word, introduced by the admonition, 'Do not pray as the hypocrites; but as the Lord commanded in his gospel, thus pray ye.' The Prayer concludes with a doxology consisting of two terms, 'for thine is the power and the glory for ever'. There then follows (in 8.3) the advice, 'Three times a day, pray thus.' Here, in the earliest period, regular use of the Lord's Prayer is therefore presupposed, though without any apparent connection with the sacraments. Yet this impression is false. The matter becomes clear if one notes the context in which the Lord's Prayer stands in the *Didache*.[5] The *Didache* begins with instruction in the 'Two Ways', the Way of Life and the Way of Death (chapters 1-6); this teaching no doubt belonged to the instruction of candidates for baptism. Chapter 7 treats baptism; and then begin the sections which are important for those who are baptized: fasting and prayer (including the Lord's Prayer) are treated in chapter 8, the Lord's Supper in chapters 9-10, and church organization and church discipline in chapters 11-15. For us it is important to note

---

[4] J.-P. Audet, *La Didachè: Instructions des Apôtres* (Études Bibliques), Paris 1958, p. 219.

[5] A. Seeberg, *Die vierte Bitte des Vaterunsers*, Rostock 1914, pp. 13f., reprinted in R. Seeberg ed., *D. Alfred Seeberg. Worte des Gedächtnisses an den Heimgegangenen und Arbeiten aus seinem Nachlass*, Leipzig 1916, pp. 69-82; T. W. Manson, 'The Lord's Prayer', pp. 101f.

that the Lord's Prayer and the Lord's Supper follow upon baptism. Thereby the point we made at the beginning is corroborated: the Lord's Prayer was intended in the early church—beginning already in the first century, as we can now add—only for those who were full members of the church.

All this leads to a very important result which, again, T. W. Manson has pointed out most lucidly.[6] Whereas nowadays the Lord's Prayer is understood as a common property of all people, it was otherwise in the earliest times. As one of the most holy treasures of the church, the Lord's Prayer, together with the Lord's Supper, was reserved for full members, and it was not disclosed to those who stood outside. It was a privilege to be allowed to pray it. How great was the reverence and awe which surrounded it is best seen by the introductory formulae found both in the liturgies of the East and in those of the West. In the East, in the so-called Liturgy of St John Chrysostom, which even today is still the usual form of the mass among the Greek and Russian Orthodox, the priest prays, at the introduction of the Lord's Prayer, 'And make us worthy, O Lord, that we joyously and without presumption may make bold to invoke Thee, the heavenly God, as Father, and to say: Our Father.' The formula in the Roman mass in the West is similar: 'We make bold to say (*audemus dicere*): Our Father.'

This awesome reverence before the Lord's Prayer was a reality in the ancient church, which, unfortunately, has been lost to us today for the most part. That should disquiet us. We ought therefore to ask ourselves whether we can again discover why the early church surrounded the Lord's Prayer with such reverence, so that they said, 'We make bold to say: Our Father.' Perhaps we may regain an inkling of the basis for this awe if, with the aid of the results of recent New Testament research, we try to discover, as best we can, how Jesus himself meant the words of the Lord's Prayer.

2. THE EARLIEST TEXT OF THE LORD'S PRAYER

We must first clear up a preliminary question, namely that of the earliest text of the Lord's Prayer. The Lord's Prayer has been handed down to us at two places in the New Testament, in Matthew as part of the Sermon on the Mount (Matt. 6.9-13), and

[6] *Ibid.*

in Luke in chapter 11 (Luke 11.2-4). Before trying to consider the original meaning of the petitions of the Prayer, we must face the strange fact that the two evangelists, Matthew and Luke, transmit it in slightly different wordings. It is true that in the Authorized Version the differences are limited, the main divergence being that in Luke the doxology is absent, i.e., the concluding words: 'For thine is the kingdom, and the power, and the glory, for ever.' Likewise in the older editions of the Luther Bible in German the two versions agree with one another, save for trivial variations and the absence of the doxology in Luke. But as a matter of fact, the divergences are greater than this. In the Revised Standard Version or in the New English Bible translation, just as in the Zürcherbibel, we read a form of the Lord's Prayer at Luke 11.2-4 which is briefer than that found in Matthew.

It is well known that in the last one hundred and twenty years research into the oldest text-form of the New Testament has gone forward with great energy, first in Germany, and then in England, and in the last decades also in America, and admirable results have been achieved in recovering the oldest text. This work was triggered by the discovery of numerous manuscripts of the New Testament, often very ancient ones. In 1963 the number of New Testament manuscripts in Greek alone totalled 4,903. By comparing and classifying these manuscripts, scholars have succeeded in working out an earlier text than that which the translators of the AV or Luther possessed. While for the 1611 translators or for Luther the text-form was available much as it had been developed at the end of the fourth century in the Byzantine church, we today know the text of approximately the second century. One can say, without exaggeration, that this chapter in research is essentially concluded and that we today have attained the best possible Greek text of the New Testament. With regard to the Lord's Prayer, the results are as follows: At the time when the gospels of Matthew and of Luke were being composed (about AD 75-85) the Lord's Prayer was being transmitted in two forms which agreed with each other in essentials, but which differed in the fact that the one was longer than the other. The longer form appears in Matthew 6.9-13 and also, with insignificant variations, in the *Didache*, at 8.2; the briefer form appears at Luke 11.2-4.

While the Matthaean version agrees with that form which is familiar to us, a form of the Prayer with seven petitions (only the doxology is lacking in Matthew[7]), the Lucan version has only five petitions according to the oldest manuscripts. It runs:

> Father,
> Hallowed be thy name.
> Thy kingdom come.
> Give us each day our bread for tomorrow.
> And forgive us our sins, for we also forgive
>   everyone who is indebted to us.
> And let us not fall into temptation.

Two questions now arise. (1) How is it that about the year AD 75 the Lord's Prayer was being transmitted and prayed in two forms which diverged from one another? And (2), which of the two forms is to be regarded as the original?

(a) The two forms

The answer to the first question, namely, how it is to be explained that the Lord's Prayer was transmitted in two forms, emerges when we observe the context in which the Lord's Prayer occurs in Matthew and Luke. In both cases the Lord's Prayer occurs with words of Jesus which treat prayer.

In Matthew we read, in the section 6.1-18, a discussion which opposes the type of piety practised in the lay circles which formed the Pharisaic movement. The Lord reproves the fact that they offer their alms (6.2-4) and their prayers (6.5f.) and conduct their fasts (6.16-18) publicly for show and thus use them to serve their craving for approval and to feed their own self-conceit. In contrast he demands of his disciples that their almsgiving and prayer and fasting shall take place in secret, so that only God beholds it. The three units are symmetrically constructed: in each instance false and right conduct are contrasted with each other through two 'when'—clauses. But the middle unit, which deals with prayer (6.5f.), is expanded through three further words of Jesus about prayer, so that the following structure arose: (*a*) The foundation was provided by the admonition of Jesus that his disciples were not to be like the Pharisees who arrange things so that they find themselves in the midst of the tumult of the market place when trumpet blasts from the Temple announce the hour of prayer, with the result that, evidently to their complete surprise,

---

[7] On the doxology, see further below, pp. 106f.

they have to pray amid the throng of men. No, Jesus' disciples are to pray behind closed doors, even, if need be, in so worldly a place as the storeroom (Greek, ταμεῖον; RSV, 'your room'; 6.5f.). (*b*) To this there is joined Jesus' admonition not to 'heap up empty phrases as the Gentiles do'. As children of the heavenly Father, his disciples do not need to employ 'many words' (6.7f.). (*c*) The Lord's Prayer follows as an example of brief prayer (6.9-13). As a matter of fact, this prayer from the Lord is distinguished from most prayers in ancient Judaism by its brevity. (*d*) Emphatic in its position at the end of this middle section is a saying of Jesus about inner disposition in prayer, a saying which connects with the petition on forgiveness: only he who is himself ready to forgive has the right to petition God for forgiveness (6.14f.). We thus have before us in Matthew 6.5-15 a catechism on prayer, put together from words of Jesus, a catechism which would be employed in the instruction of the newly baptized.

In Luke, too, the Lord's Prayer occurs in such a catechism on prayer (Luke 11.1-13). This indicates how important the primitive church considered the instruction of its members in the right kind of prayer. In Luke, however, the catechism on prayer is of a very different sort from that found in Matthew. But it too falls into four parts: (*a*) There is prefixed a picture of the Lord at prayer as a prototype for all Christian prayer, and the request of the disciples, 'Lord, teach us to pray' (11.1). Jesus fulfils this request with the Lord's Prayer (11.2-4). (*b*) The parable about the man who knocks on his friend's door at midnight is added here. In its present context it presents an admonition to persist in prayer, even if one's prayer is not heard immediately (11.5-8). (*c*) The same admonition then follows in imperative form: 'Ask, and it will be given you' (11.9f.). (*d*) The conclusion is formed by the picture of the father who 'gives good gifts' to his children (11.11-13).

The differences in these two primers on prayer are to be explained by the fact that they are directed at very different groups of people. The Matthaean catechism on prayer is addressed to people who have learned to pray in childhood but whose prayer stands in danger of becoming a routine. The Lucan catechism on prayer, on the other hand, is addressed to people who must for the first time learn to pray and whose courage to pray must be roused. It is clear that Matthew is transmitting to us instruction on prayer directed at Jewish-Christians, Luke at Gentile-Christians. About AD 75, therefore, the Lord's Prayer was a fixed element in instructions on prayer in all Christendom, in the Jewish-Christian as well as in the Gentile-Christian church. Both churches, different as their situations were, were at one on this point: that a Christian learned, from the Lord's Prayer, how to pray.

For our question then of how it is to be explained that in Matthew and Luke we find two forms of the Lord's Prayer which vary from each other, the conclusion is that the variations can in no case be traced back to the caprice of the evangelists—no author would have dared to make such alteration in the Prayer on his own—but rather that the variations are to be seen within a broader context: we have before us the wording for the Prayer from two churches, that is, different liturgical wordings of the Lord's Prayer. Each of the evangelists transmits to us the wording of the Lord's Prayer as it was prayed in his church at that time.

(b) *The original form*

Now we can deal with the second question: which of the two forms is to be regarded as the original?

If we compare the two texts carefully, the most striking divergence is the difference in length. The Lucan form (see p. 87) is shorter than that of Matthew at three places. First, the invocation is shorter. Luke says only 'Father', or properly 'dear Father', in Greek πάτερ, in Aramaic *abba*, whereas Matthew says, according to the pious and reverent form of Palestinian invocation, 'Our Father who art in heaven'. Second, whereas Matthew and Luke agree in the first two petitions—the 'Thou-petitions' ('Hallowed be thy name, thy kingdom come')—there follows in Matthew a third 'Thou-petition': 'Thy will be done in earth, as it is in heaven.' Third, in Matthew the last of the following 'We-petitions' has an antithesis. Luke has only: 'And let us not fall into temptation', but Matthew adds: 'but deliver us from evil'.

Now, if we ask which form is the original—the longer form of Matthew or the shorter form of Luke—the decisive observation, which has not yet been mentioned, is the following: the shorter form of Luke is completely contained in the longer form of Matthew. This makes it very probable that the Matthaean form is an expanded one, for according to all that we know about the tendency of liturgical texts to conform to certain laws in their transmission, in a case where the shorter version is contained in the longer one, the shorter text is to be regarded as original. No one would have dared to shorten a sacred text like the Lord's Prayer and to leave out two petitions if they had formed part of the original tradition. On the contrary, the reverse is amply attested, that in the early period, before wordings were fixed, liturgical texts were elaborated, expanded, and enriched. This conclusion, that the Matthaean version represents an expansion, is confirmed by three supplementary observations. First, the three expansions which we find in Matthew, as compared with Luke, are always found toward the end of a section of the prayer—the first at the end of the address, the second at the end of the 'Thou-petitions', the third at the end of the 'We-petitions'. This again is exactly in accordance with what we find elsewhere in the growth of liturgical texts; they show a proclivity for sonorous expansions at the end.

Second, it is of further significance that in Matthew the stylistic structure is more consistently carried through. Three 'Thou-petitions' in Matthew correspond to the three 'We-petitions' (the sixth and seventh petitions in Matthew were regarded as one petition). The third 'We-petition', which in Luke seems abrupt because of its brevity, is in Matthew assimilated to the first two 'We-petitions'. To spell this out, the first two 'We-petitions' show a parallelism:

> Our bread for tomorrow / give us today.[8]
> Do Thou forgive us / as we forgive.

In Luke, however, the third 'We-petition' is shorter, apparently intentionally:

> And lead us not into temptation.

But Matthew offers a parallelism here too:

> And lead us not into temptation / but deliver us from evil.

This endeavour to produce parallelism in lines (*parallelismus membrorum*) is a characteristic of liturgical tradition. One can see the point especially well if one compares the various versions of the words of institution at the Lord's Supper.

Third, a final point in favour of the originality of the Lucan

---

[8] On this two-part (or two half-lines) division of the petition for daily bread, see below, pp. 91ff. and 99f.

version is the reappearance of the brief form of address 'dear Father' (*abba*) in the prayers of the earliest Christians, as we see from Rom. 8.15 and Gal. 4.6. Matthew has a sonorous address, 'Our Father who art in heaven', such as corresponded to pious Jewish-Palestinian custom. We shall see that the simple *abba* was a unique note in Jesus' own prayers. Thus we must conclude that this plain *abba* was the original address.

All these observations lead us, then, in the same direction. The common substance of both texts, which is identical with its Lucan form, is the oldest text. The Gentile-Christian church has handed down the Lord's Prayer without change, whereas the Jewish-Christian church, which lived in a world of rich liturgical tradition and used a variety of prayer forms, has enriched the Lord's Prayer liturgically.[9] Because the form transmitted by Matthew was the more richly elaborated one, it soon permeated the whole church; we saw above[10] that the *Didache* presents this form too.

Of course, we must be cautious with our conclusions. The possibility remains that Jesus himself spoke the 'Our Father' on different occasions in a slightly differing form, a shorter one and a longer one. But perhaps it would be safer to say that the shorter Lucan form is in all probability the oldest one, whereas Matthew gives us the earliest evidence that the Lord's Prayer was used liturgically in worship. In any case, the chief thing is that both texts agree in the decisive elements.

Nonetheless the question about the original form of the Lord's Prayer is still not completely answered. We have thus far directed our attention only to the varying lengths of the two versions. But in the lines where they share a common wording these versions also exhibit certain—admittedly, not very significant—variations, specifically in the second part, the 'We-petitions'. To these differences we now turn briefly.

The first 'We-petition', for daily bread, reads in Matthew, 'Give us this day our bread for the morrow'. As we shall see later, the contrast, 'this day—for the morrow', sets the whole tone for the verse. In Luke, on the other hand, it reads, 'give us each day our bread for the morrow'. Here the term 'this day' is expanded into

---

[9] This was done gradually, as can be gathered from the fact that in Matthew the word 'heaven' is in the plural in the address (semitic usage), whereas it is in the singular in the third petition (Greek usage).

[10] P. 86.

'each day'; the petition is thereby broadened into a generalized saying, with the consequence that the antithesis 'this day—for the morrow' drops out. Moreover, in Luke the Greek word for 'give' now had to be expressed with the present imperative (δίδου, literally 'keep on giving!'), whereas elsewhere throughout the Prayer the aorist imperative is used, which denotes a single action. Matthew also has the aorist imperative in this petition: δός, 'give'! From all this it may be concluded that the Matthaean form of the petition for daily bread is the older one.

In the second 'We-petition', for forgiveness, Matthew has 'Forgive us our debts', while Luke has 'Forgive us our sins'. Now it was a peculiarity of Jesus' mother tongue, Aramaic, that the word *ḥobha* was used for 'sin', though it properly means a debt, 'money owed'. Matthew translates the word quite literally with 'debts', ὀφειλήματα, a word which is not usual in Greek for 'sin'; this enables one to see that the Lord's Prayer goes back to an Aramaic wording. In the Lucan version, the word 'debts' is represented by the usual Greek word for 'sins', ἁμαρτίαι; but the wording in the next clause ('for we ourselves forgive everyone who is *indebted* to us') makes it evident that in the initial clause 'debts' had originally appeared. In this case, too, Matthew therefore has the older wording.

The same picture results when one focuses attention on yet a final variation in wording. We read in Matthew (literally translated), 'as we also have forgiven (ἀφήκαμεν) our debtors', while in Luke we read, 'for we also ourselves forgive (ἀφίομεν) everyone who is indebted to us'. When we ask which formulation is the older, the past tense in Matthew or the present tense form in Luke, it is readily seen that Matthew has the more difficult form, and in such cases the more difficult form is to be regarded as the more original. Matthew's is the more difficult form, because his wording ('as we have forgiven') could lead to the mistaken impression that not only must our forgiving precede forgiveness on God's part, but that it also provides the standard for God's forgiving us: 'forgive us thus, as we have forgiven'. In actuality, however, there lies behind Matthew's past tense form what is called in Semitic grammar a *perfectum praesens*, a 'present perfect', which refers to an action occurring here and now. The correct translation of the Matthaean form would therefore run, 'as we also herewith forgive our debtors'. By its choice of the present tense form, Luke's version was intended to exclude a misunderstanding among Greek-speaking Christians, since it says (and this catches the sense): 'for we also ourselves forgive everyone who is indebted to us'. Moreover, in the Lucan form, the petition on forgiveness is broadened by the addition of the word 'everyone', which represents a sharpening of the meaning, in that it permits no exceptions in our forgiving.

Comparison of the wording of the two forms of the Lord's Prayer therefore shows that, over against Matthew, the Lucan form has been assimilated at several points to Greek linguistic usage. Viewed as a whole, our results may be summarized thus: the Lucan version has preserved the oldest form with respect to *length*, but the Matthaean text is more original with regard to *wording*.

In our consideration of the petition for forgiveness, we have just observed that the Matthaean phrase 'our debts' enables one to see that the Lord's Prayer, which is of course preserved for us only in Greek, goes back to an original Aramaic version. As we shall see later,[11] this observation is confirmed by the fact that the two 'Thou-petitions' relate to an Aramaic prayer, the *Kaddish*. When one attempts to put the Lord's Prayer back into Aramaic, Jesus' mother tongue, the conclusion begins to emerge that, like the Psalter, it is couched in liturgical language. Even the person who brings no knowledge of the Semitic languages to his reading of the following attempt at retranslation can easily spot the characteristic features of this solemn language. We should note three features especially: parallelism, the two-beat rhythm, and the rhyme in lines two and four, which is scarcely accidental. The Lord's Prayer in Jesus' tongue sounded something like this (the accents designate the two-beat rhythm)[12]:

---

[11] Below, p. 98.

[12] On the problem of the original Aramaic form and attempts at retranslation of the Lord's Prayer into Aramaic, cf. C. C. Torrey, 'The Translations made from the Original Aramaic Gospels', in: *Studies in the History of Religions presented to Crawford Howell Toy by Pupils, Colleagues and Friends*, New York 1912, pp. 309-17; *id.*, *The Four Gospels*, New York 1933, p. 292; E. Littmann, 'Torreys Buch über die vier Evangelien', *ZNW* 34 (1935), pp. 20-34, especially pp. 29f.; C. F. Burney, *The Poetry of Our Lord*, Oxford 1925, pp. 112f.; G. Dalman, *Die Worte Jesu*, I², Leipzig 1930, pp. 283-365 (Appendix on 'Das Vaterunser' which is not in the *ET* of the 1st edition. *The Words of Jesus*, Edinburgh 1902); K. G. Kuhn, *Achtzehngebet und Vaterunser und der Reim* (WUNT 1), Tübingen 1950, pp. 32f.

> *'Abbā*
> *yithqaddásh sheʰmákh | tethé malkhuthákh*
> *laḥmán deʰlimḥár | habh lán yoma dhén*
> *usheʰbhoq lán ḥobhaín | keʰdhisheʰbháqnan leʰḥayyabhaín*
> *weʰla thaʿelínnan leʰnisyón.*

3. THE MEANING OF THE LORD'S PRAYER

Having considered what can be said about the original wording, we are prepared to face the main question. What was, as far as we can judge, the original meaning?

Luke reports that Jesus gave the Lord's Prayer to his disciples on a quite specific occasion.

> He was praying in a certain place, and when he ceased, one of his disciples said to him, 'Lord, teach us to pray, as John taught his disciples.' (11.1)

That the unnamed disciple appealed to the example of John the Baptist is important for our understanding of the Lord's Prayer, since we know that at the time of Jesus individual religious groups were marked by their own prayer customs and forms. This was true of the Pharisees, the Essenes, and, as we perceive from Luke 11.1, the disciples of John as well. A particular custom in prayer expressed the particular relationship with God which bound the individuals together. The request at Luke 11.1 therefore shows that Jesus' disciples recognized themselves as a community, or more exactly as the community of the age of salvation, and that they requested of Jesus a prayer which would bind them together and identify them, in that it would bring to expression their chief concern. As a matter of fact, the Lord's Prayer is the clearest and, in spite of its terseness, the richest summary of Jesus' proclamation which we possess. When the Lord's Prayer was given to the disciples, prayer in Jesus' name began (John 14.13f.; 15.16; 16.23).[13]

The structure of the Lord's Prayer is simple and transparent. We present once again what is presumably the oldest wording (following the short form according to Luke, but where there are minor variations of wording that of Matthew):

> Dear Father,
> Hallowed be thy name.
> Thy kingdom come.

[13] K. H. Rengstorf, *Das Evangelium nach Lukas* (NTD 3)[9], Göttingen 1962, p. 144.

Our bread for tomorrow / give us today.
And forgive us our debts / as we also herewith forgive our debtors.
And let us not succumb to temptation.

The structure of the Lord's Prayer then consists of: (1) the address; (2) two 'Thou-petitions' in parallel (in Matthew, three); (3) two 'We-petitions' in parallel, both forming, as we shall see, an antithesis; (4) the concluding request. We also observe what seems to be an apparently insignificant point: while the two 'Thou-petitions' stand side-by-side without any 'and', the two parallel 'We-petitions' are connected by an 'and'.

(a) The address 'Dear Father' (abba)

When we trace back to its earliest beginnings the history of the invocation of God as father, we have the feeling of descending into a mine in which new and unexpected treasures are disclosed one after another. It is surprising to see that already in the ancient Orient, as early as the third and second millennia BC, we find the deity addressed as father. We find this title for the first time in Sumerian prayers, long before the time of Moses and the prophets, and there already the word 'father' does not merely refer to the deity as procreator and ancestor of the king and of the people and as powerful lord, but it also has quite another significance: it is used for the 'merciful, gracious father, in whose hand the life of the whole land lies' (a hymn from Ur to the moon god Sin).[14] For Orientals, the word 'father', as applied to God, thus encompasses, from earliest times, something of what the word 'mother' signifies among us.

When we turn to the Old Testament, we find that God is only seldom spoken of as father—in fact only on fourteen occasions, but all these are important. God is Israel's father, but now not mythologically as procreator or ancestor, but as the one who elected, delivered, and saved his people Israel by mighty deeds in history. This designation of God as father in the Old Testament comes to full fruition, however, in the message of the prophets. God is Israel's father. But the prophets must make constant accusation against God's people that Israel has not given God the honour which a son should give to his father.

[14] See J. B. Pritchard, *Ancient Near Eastern Texts relating to the Old Testament*[2], Princeton, New Jersey, 1955, p. 385.

> A son honours his father,
>> and a servant his master.
> If then I am a father,
>> where is my honour?
> And if I am a master,
>> where is my fear?
>> says the Lord of hosts.
>>> (Mal. 1.6; cf. Deut. 32.5f.; Jer. 3.19f.)

And Israel's answer to this rebuke is a confession of sin and the ever-reiterated cry, *Abhinu atta*, 'Thou art our father' (Isa. 63.15f.; 64.7f.; Jer. 3.4). And God's reply to this cry is mercy beyond all understanding:

> Is Ephraim my dear son?
> Is he my darling child? . . .
> Therefore my heart yearns for him;
> I must have mercy on him,
>> says the Lord. (Jer. 31.20)

Can there be any deeper dimension to the term 'father' than this compulsive, forgiving mercy which is beyond comprehension?

When we turn to Jesus' preaching, the answer must be: Yes, here there is something quite new, absolutely new—the word *abba*. From the prayer in Gethsemane, Mark 14.36, we learn that Jesus addressed God with this word, and this point is confirmed not only by Rom. 8.15 and Gal. 4.6, but also by the striking oscillation of the forms for the vocative 'O father' in the Greek text of the gospels, an oscillation which is to be explained only through the fact that the Aramaic term *abba* lies behind all such passages. With the help of my assistants I have examined the prayer literature of ancient Judaism—a large, rich literature, all too little explored. The result of this examination was that in no place in this immense literature is this invocation of God as *abba* to be found. How is this to be explained? The church fathers Chrysostom, Theodore of Mopsuestia, and Theodoret of Cyrus who originated from Antioch (where the populace spoke the West Syrian dialect of Aramaic) and who probably had Aramaic-speaking nurses, testify unanimously that *abba* was the address of the small child to his father. And the Talmud confirms this when it says: 'When a child experiences the taste of wheat [i.e. when it is weaned], it learns to say *abba* and *imma* ['dear father' and 'dear mother'].'[15] *Abba* and *imma* are thus originally the first sounds

[15] *b. Ber.* 40a; *b. Sanh.* 70b.

which the child stammers. In Jesus' days they were no longer restricted to children's talk; they were also used by grown-up sons and daughters to address their parents. Yet their humble origin was not forgotten. *Abba* was an everyday word, a homely family-word. No Jew would have dared to address God in this manner. Jesus did it always, in all his prayers which are handed down to us, with one single exception, the cry from the cross: 'My God, my God, why hast thou forsaken me?' (Mark 15.34; Matt. 27.46); here the term of address for God was prescribed by the fact that Jesus was quoting Ps. 22.1. Jesus thus spoke with God as a child speaks with his father, simply, intimately, securely. But his invocation of God as *abba* is not to be understood merely psychologically, as a step toward growing apprehension of God. Rather we learn from Matt. 11.27 that Jesus himself viewed this form of address for God as the heart of that revelation which had been granted him by the Father. In this term *abba* the ultimate mystery of his mission and his authority is expressed. He, to whom the Father had granted full knowledge of God, has the messianic prerogative of addressing him with the familiar address of a son. This term *abba* is an *ipsissima vox*[16] of Jesus and contains *in nuce* his message and his claim to have been sent from the Father.

The final point, and the most astonishing of all, however, has yet to be mentioned: in the Lord's Prayer Jesus authorizes his disciples to repeat the word *abba* after him. He gives them a share in his sonship and empowers them, as his disciples, to speak with their heavenly Father in just such a familiar, trusting way as a child would with his father. Yes, he goes so far as to say that it is this new relationship which first opens the doors to God's reign: 'Truly, I say to you, unless you become like children again,[17] you will not find entrance into the kingdom of God' (Matt. 18.3). Children can say '*abba*'! Only he who, through Jesus, lets himself be given the childlike trust which resides in the word *abba* finds his way into the kingdom of God. This the apostle Paul also understood; he says twice that there is no surer sign or guarantee of the possession of the Holy Spirit and of the gift of sonship than this, that a man makes bold to repeat this one word, 'Abba, dear Father'

---

[16] *Ipsissima vox* of Jesus = Jesus' own original way of speaking (cf. 'Characteristics of the *ipsissima vox Jesu*', below, pp. 108-115).

[17] As it might be translated from the Aramaic. The translation which is familiar to us remains possible: 'unless you turn and become like children'.

(Rom. 8.15; Gal. 4.6). Perhaps at this point we get some inkling why the use of the Lord's Prayer was not a commonplace in the early church and why it was spoken with such reverence and awe: 'Make us worthy, O Lord, that we joyously and without presumption may make bold to invoke Thee, the heavenly God, as Father, and to say, Our Father.'

(b) The two 'Thou-petitions'

The first words which the child says to his heavenly Father are, 'Hallowed be thy name Thy kingdom come.' These two petitions are not only parallel in structure, but they also correspond to one another in content. They recall the *Kaddish* ('Holy'), an ancient Aramaic prayer which formed the conclusion of the service in the synagogue and with which Jesus was no doubt familiar from childhood. What is probably the oldest form of this prayer (later expanded) runs:

> Exalted and hallowed be his great name
>   in the world which he created according to his will.
> May he let his kingdom rule
>   in your lifetime and in your days and in the lifetime
>   of the whole house of Israel, speedily and soon.
> And to this, say: amen.

It is from this connection with the *Kaddish* that we can explain the way in which the two 'Thou-petitions' (in contrast with the two parallel 'We-petitions') stand alongside each other without any connecting word; for in the earliest texts of the *Kaddish* the two petitions about the hallowing of the name and the coming of the kingdom appear not to be connected by an 'and'.

Comparison with the *Kaddish* also shows that the two petitions are eschatological. They make entreaty for the revelation of God's eschatological kingdom. Every accession to power by an earthly ruler is accompanied by homage in words and gestures. So it will be when God enters upon his rule. Then men will do homage to him, hallowing his name: 'Holy, holy, holy, is the Lord God Almighty, who was and is and is to come' (Rev. 4.8); then they will all prostrate themselves at the feet of the King of kings, 'We give thanks to thee, Lord God Almighty, who art and who wast, that thou hast taken thy great power and begun to reign' (Rev. 11.17). The two 'Thou-petitions', to which in Matthew there is added yet a third one of like meaning ('Thy will be done, on earth as it is in heaven'), thus make entreaty for the final consummation. Their contents strike the same note as the prayer of the early church, *Maranatha* (I Cor. 16.22), 'Come, Lord Jesus' (Rev. 22.20). They seek the hour in which God's profaned and misused name will be glorified and his reign revealed, in accordance with the promise, 'I will vindicate the holiness of my great name, which has been profaned among the nations, and which you have profaned among them; and the nations will know that I am the Lord, says the Lord God, when through you I vindicate my holiness before their eyes' (Ezek. 36.23).

These petitions are a cry out of the depths of distress. Out of a world which is enslaved under the rule of evil and in which Christ and Antichrist are locked in conflict, Jesus' disciples, seemingly a prey of evil and death and Satan, lift their eyes to the Father and cry out for the revelation of God's glory. But at the same time these petitions are an expression of absolute certainty. He who prays thus, takes seriously God's promise, in spite of all the demonic powers, and puts himself completely in God's hands, with imperturbable trust: 'Thou wilt complete Thy glorious work, *abba*, Father.'

These are the same words which the Jewish community prays in the synagogue at the end of the service in the *Kaddish*; yet the two 'Thou-petitions' are not the same as the *Kaddish*, in spite of the similar wording. There is a great difference. In the *Kaddish* the prayer is by a congregation which stands in the darkness of the present age and asks for the consummation. In the Lord's Prayer, though similar words are used, a congregation is praying which knows that the turning point has already come, because God has already begun his saving work. This congregation now makes supplication for full revelation of what has already been granted.

(c) The two 'We-petitions'

The two 'We-petitions', for daily bread and for forgiveness, hang together as closely as the two 'Thou-petitions'. This connection of the two 'We-petitions' with one another is seen immediately in the structure through the fact that both of them, in contrast to the 'Thou-petitions', consist of *two* half-lines each:

> Our bread for tomorrow / give us today.
> And forgive us our debts / as we also
>   herewith forgive our debtors.

If it is correct that the two 'Thou-petitions' recall the *Kaddish*, then we must conclude that in the Lord's Prayer the accent lies completely on the new material which Jesus added, that is, on the two 'We-petitions'. They form the real heart of the Lord's Prayer, to which the two 'Thou-petitions' lead up.

(*a*) The first of the two 'We-petitions' asks for daily bread (Greek, ἄρτος ἐπιούσιος). The Greek word ἐπιούσιος, which Luther rendered as 'täglich' ('daily') and Tyndale in 1525 and the Authorized Version as 'daily', has been the object of lengthy discussion which is not yet finally settled. In my opinion, the decisive fact is that the church father Jerome (*c.* AD 342-420) tells us that in the lost Aramaic *Gospel of the Nazarenes* the term *maḥar* appears, meaning 'tomorrow', that here therefore the reference was to bread 'for tomorrow'.[18] Now it is true that this *Gospel of the Nazarenes* is not older than our first three gospels; rather it rests on our Gospel of Matthew. Nonetheless the Aramaic wording of the Lord's Prayer in the *Gospel of the Nazarenes* ('bread for tomorrow') must be older than the *Gospel of the Nazarenes* and older even than our gospels. For in first-century Palestine the Lord's Prayer was prayed in uninterrupted usage in Aramaic, and a person translating the Gospel of Matthew into Aramaic naturally did not translate the Lord's Prayer as he did the rest of the text. Instead, when the translator came to Matt. 6.9-13, he of course stopped translating; he simply wrote down the holy words in the form in which he prayed them day by day. In other words, the Aramaic-speaking Jewish-Christians, among whom the Lord's Prayer lived on in its original Aramaic wording in unbroken usage since the days of Jesus, prayed, 'Our bread for tomorrow give us today.'

Jerome tells us even more. He adds a remark telling how the phrase, 'bread for tomorrow' was understood. He says: 'In the so called Gospel according to the Hebrews [i.e., the Nazarenes] . . . . found *maḥar*, which means "for tomorrow", so that the sense is "Our bread for tomorrow—that is, our future bread—give us today." ' As a matter of fact, in ancient Judaism *maḥar*, 'tomorrow' meant not only the next day but also the great Tomorrow, the final consummation. Accordingly, Jerome is saying, the 'bread for tomorrow' was not meant as earthly bread but as the bread o

---

[18] *Commentary on Matthew*, on Matt. 6.11 (text, E. Klostermann *Apocrypha* II², Kleine Texte 8, Berlin 1929, p. 7; *ET*, M. R. James, *Th Apocryphal New Testament*, Oxford 1924, p. 4).

ife. Further, we know from the ancient translations of the Lord's Prayer, both in the East and in the West, that in the early church this eschatological understanding—'bread of the age of salvation', 'bread of life', 'heavenly manna'—was the familiar, if not the predominant interpretation of the phrase 'bread for tomorrow'. Since primeval times, the bread of life and the water of life have been symbols of paradise, an epitome of the fullness of all God's material and spiritual gifts. It is this bread—symbol, image, and fulfilment of the age of salvation—to which Jesus is referring when he says that in the consummation he will eat and drink with his disciples (Luke 22.30) and that he will gird himself and serve them at table (Luke 12.37) with the bread which has been broken and the cup which has been blessed (cf. Matt. 26.29). The eschatological thrust of all the other petitions in the Lord's Prayer speaks for the fact that the petition for bread has an eschatological sense too, i.e., that it entreats God for the bread of life.

This interpretation may perhaps be a surprise or even a disappointment for us. For so many people it is important that at least *one* petition in the Lord's Prayer should lead into everyday life, the petition for daily bread. Is that to be taken away from us? Is that not an impoverishment? No, in reality, application of the petition about bread to the bread of life is a great enrichment. It would be a gross misunderstanding if one were to suppose that here there is a 'spiritualizing', after the manner of Greek philosophy, and that there is a distinction made between 'earthly' and 'heavenly' bread. For Jesus, earthly bread and the bread of life are not antithetical. In the realm of God's kingship he viewed all earthly things as hallowed. His disciples belong to God's new age; they are snatched away from the age of death (Matt. 8.22). This fact manifests itself in their life down to the last details. It expresses itself in their words (Matt. 5.21f., 33-37), in their looks (5.28), in the way they greet men on the street (5.47); it expresses itself also in their eating and drinking. For the disciples of Jesus there are no longer 'clean' or 'unclean' foods. 'Nothing that a man eats can make him "unclean"' (Mark 7.15); all that God provides is blessed. This 'hallowing of life' is most clearly illustrated by the picture of Jesus at table for a meal. The bread which he proffered when he sat at table with publicans and sinners was everyday bread, and yet it was more: it was bread of life. The bread which he broke for his disciples at the Last Supper was earthly bread, and yet it was more: his body given for many in death, the gift of a portion in the atoning power of his death. Every meal his disciples had with him was a usual eating and drinking, and yet it was more: a meal of salvation, a messianic meal, image and anticipation of the meal at the consummation, because he was the master of the house. This remained true in the primitive church: their daily fellowship meals were the customary meals for sustenance, and yet at the same time they were a 'Lord's supper' (I Cor. 11.20) which mediated fellowship with him and linked in fellowship with one another those sitting at table (I Cor. 10.16f.). In the same way, for all his followers, every meal is a meal in his presence. He is the host who fills the hungry and thirsty with the fullness of his blessings.

It is in this sense too that the petition about 'bread for tomorrow' is intended. It does not sever everyday life and the kingdom of God from one another, but it encompasses the totality of life. It embraces everything that Jesus' disciples need for body and soul. It includes 'daily bread', but it does not content itself with that. It asks that amid the secularity of everyday life the powers and gifts of God's coming age may be active in all that Jesus' disciples do in word and deed. One can flatly say that this petition for the bread of life makes entreaty for the hallowing of everyday life.

Only when one has perceived that the petition asks for bread in the fullest sense, for the bread of life, does the antithesis between 'for tomorrow' and 'today' gain its full significance. This word 'today', which stands at the end of the petition, gets the real stress. In a world enslaved under Satan, in a world where God is remote, in a world of hunger and thirst, the disciples of Jesus dare to utter this word 'today'—even now, even here, already on this day, give us the bread of life. Jesus grants to them, as the children of God, the privilege of stretching forth their hands to grasp the glory of the consummation, to fetch it down, to 'believe it down', to pray it down—right into their poor lives, even now, even here, today.

(b) Even now—this is also the meaning of the petition for forgiveness, 'And forgive us our debts as we also herewith forgive our debtors.' This request looks toward the great reckoning which the world is approaching, the disclosure of God's majesty n the final judgment. Jesus' disciples know how they are involved n sin and debt; they know that only God's gracious forgiveness can save them from the wrath to come. But they ask not only for nercy in the hour of the last judgment—rather they ask, again, hat God might grant them forgiveness already today. Through esus their lord, they, as his disciples, belong to the age of salvation. The age of the Messiah is an age of forgiveness. Forgiveness is the one great gift of this age. 'Grant us, dear Father,' hey pray, 'this one great gift of the Messiah's time, already in this day and in this place.'

This second 'We-petition' also has two parts, two half-lines, ike the petition for daily bread. There is an antithesis, contrasting 'Thou' and 'we': 'forgive us our debts as we forgive our debtors.' The second half-line, about forgiving our debtors, makes a quite striking reference to human activity. Such a reference occurs only at this point in the Lord's Prayer, so that one can see from his fact how important this second clause was to Jesus. The word 'as' (in 'as we forgive') does not imply a comparison; how could Jesus' disciples compare their poor forgiving with God's mercy? Rather, the 'as' introduces a declaration, for, as we have already seen,[19] the correct translation from the Aramaic must be, 'as we also herewith forgive our debtors'. With these words he who prays reminds himself of his own need to forgive. Jesus again and again declared this very point, that you cannot ask God for forgiveness if you are not prepared to forgive. God can forgive only if we are ready to forgive. 'Whenever you stand praying, forgive, if you have anything against any one; so that your Father also who is in heaven may forgive you your trespasses' (Mark 11.25). At Matt. 5.23f. Jesus even goes so far as to say that he disciple is to interrupt his presentation of the offering with which he is entreating God's forgiveness, if it occurs to him that his brother holds something against him; he is to be reconciled with his brother before he completes the offering of his sacrifice. In these verses Jesus means to say that the request for God's forgiveness is false and cannot be heard by God if the disciple has not on his part previously cleared up his relationship with the brother. This willingness to forgive is, so to speak, the hand which Jesus' disciples reach out toward God's forgiveness. They say, 'O Lord, we indeed belong to the age of the Messiah, to the

---

[19] Above, pp. 92f.

age of forgiveness, and we are ready to pass on to others the forgiveness which we receive. Now grant us, dear Father, the gift of
the age of salvation, thy forgiveness. We stretch out our hands,
forgive us our debts—even now, even here, already today.'

Only when one observes that the two 'We-petitions' are both
directed toward the consummation and that they both implore its
gifts for this present time, only then does the connection between
the two 'Thou-petitions' and the two 'We-petitions' really become
clear. The two 'We-petitions' are the actualization of the 'Thou-
petitions'. The 'Thou-petitions' ask for the revelation of God's
glory. The two 'We-petitions' make bold to 'pray down' this
consummation, even here and even now.

(d) The conclusion: the Petition for Preservation

Up to this point, the petitions have been in parallel to one
another, the two 'Thou-petitions' as well as the two 'We-petitions'.
Moreover the two 'We-petitions' each consisted of two half-lines.
Hence even the form makes the concluding petition, which
consists of only a single line, stand out as abrupt and harsh:

> And let us not fall into temptation.

It also departs from the pattern of the previous petitions in that it
is the only one formulated in the negative. But all that is inten-
tional; as the contents show, this petition is supposed to stand out
as harsh and abrupt.

Two preliminary remarks about the wording must be inserted,
however. The first concerns the verb. The Greek text (literally
'and do not lead us into temptation') could be taken to imply that
God himself tempts us. The Letter of James had already rigorously
rejected this misunderstanding when—probably with direct
reference to our petition—it said, 'Let no one say when he is
tempted, "I am tempted by God"; for God cannot be tempted
with evil and he himself tempts no one' (James 1.13). How the
verb is really to be construed is shown by a very ancient Jewish
evening prayer, which Jesus could have known and with which
he perhaps makes a direct point of contact. The pertinent part
(which recurs, incidentally, almost identically worded in the
morning prayer) runs as follows:

> Lead my foot not into the power of sin,
> And bring me not into the power of iniquity,
> And not into the power of temptation,
> And not into the power of anything shameful.[20]

The juxtaposition of 'sin', 'iniquity', 'temptation', and 'anything shameful', as well as the expression 'bring into the power of', show that this Jewish evening prayer has in view not an unmediated action of God but his permission which allows something to happen. (To put it in technical grammatical terms: the causative forms which are here translated 'lead' and 'bring' have a permissive nuance.) The meaning therefore is, 'Do not permit that I fall into the hands of sin, iniquity, temptation, and anything shameful.' This evening prayer thus prays for preservation from succumbing in temptation. This is also the sense of the concluding petition of the Lord's Prayer. Hence we must render it, 'Let us not succumb to temptation.' That this reference in the final petition of the Lord's Prayer is indeed not to preservation *from* temptation but to preservation *in* temptation, is corroborated by an ancient extra-canonical saying of Jesus which, according to ancient tradition, Jesus spoke on that last evening, prior to the prayer in Gethsemane:

> No one can obtain the kingdom of heaven
> who has not passed through temptation.[21]

Here it is expressly stated that no disciple of Jesus will be spared testing through temptation; it is only the overcoming of temptation that is promised the disciple. This saying also testifies to the fact that the concluding petition of the Lord's Prayer does not request that he who prays may be spared temptation, but that God may help him to overcome it.

All this becomes fully clear when we ask, secondly, what the word 'temptation' means. This word ($\pi\epsilon\iota\rho\alpha\sigma\mu\acute{o}\varsigma$ in Greek) does not mean the little temptations or testings of everyday life, but the final great Testing which stands at the door and will extend over the whole earth—the disclosure of the mystery of evil, the revelation of the Antichrist, the abomination of desolation (when Satan stands in God's place), the final persecution and testing of God's

[20] *b. Ber.* 60b.
[21] Tertullian, *De baptismo* 20.2 (cf. J. Jeremias, *Unknown Sayings of Jesus*[2], London-Greenwich, Connecticut, 1964, pp. 73-5).

saints by pseudo-prophets and false saviours. What is in danger, is not moral integrity, but faith itself. The final trial at the end is—apostasy! Who can escape?

The concluding petition of the Lord's Prayer therefore says, 'O Lord, preserve us from falling away, from apostasy.' The Matthaean tradition also understood the petition in this way when it added the petition about final deliverance from the power of evil, which seeks to plunge men into eternal ruin: 'But deliver us from evil.'

Now, perhaps, we understand the abruptness of this last petition, why it is so brief and harsh. Jesus has summoned his disciples to ask for the consummation, when God's name will be hallowed and his kingdom come. What is more, he has encouraged them in their petitions to 'pray down' the gifts of the age of salvation into their own poor lives, even here and now. But with the soberness which characterizes all his words, Jesus warns his disciples of the danger of false enthusiasm when he calls them abruptly back to the reality of their own threatened existence by means of this concluding petition. This final petition is a cry out of the depths of distress, a resounding call for aid from a man who in affliction prays[22]: 'Dear Father, this one request grant us: preserve us from falling away from Thee.' It is surely no accident that this concluding petition has no parallels in the Old Testament.

The doxology, 'For thine is the kingdom and the power and the glory, for ever. Amen,' is lacking completely in Luke, and in Matthew it is absent from the oldest manuscripts. We encounter it first in the *Didache*.[23] But it would be a completely erroneous conclusion to suppose that the Lord's Prayer was ever prayed without some closing words of praise to God; in Palestinian practice it was completely unthinkable that a prayer would end with the word 'temptation'. Now, in Judaism prayers were often concluded with a 'seal', a sentence of praise freely formulated by the man who was praying.[24] This was doubtless also what Jesus intended with the Lord's Prayer, and what the congregation did in the earliest period: conclude the Lord's Prayer with a 'seal', i.e. a freely formulated doxology by the person praying. Afterwards, when the Lord's Prayer began to be used increasingly in

---

[22] Cf. H. Schürmann, *Das Gebet des Herrn*, p. 90.

[23] See above, p. 83f.

[24] A. Schlatter, *Der Evangelist Matthäus*, Stuttgart 1929 = ⁶1963, p. 217.

the service as a common prayer, it was felt necessary to establish a fixed formulation of the doxology.

If one ventures to summarize in *one* phrase the inexhaustible mystery of the few sentences in the Lord's Prayer, there is an expression pre-eminently suitable which New Testament research has especially busied itself with in recent decades. That phrase is 'eschatology becoming actualized' (*sich realisierende Eschatologie*). This expression denotes the age of salvation now being realized, the consummation bestowed in advance, the 'in-breaking' of God's presence into our lives. Where men dare to pray in the name of Jesus to their heavenly Father with childlike trust, that he might reveal his glory and that he might grant to them already today and in this place the bread of life and the blotting out of sins, there in the midst of the constant threat of failure and apostasy is realized, already now, the kingly rule of God over the life of his children.

Appendix

CHARACTERISTICS OF THE *IPSISSIMA VOX JESU**

IT is clear that the testimony of the Fourth Gospel to the Christ is retrospective—i.e. that it is conditioned by the internal and external situation of the church in Asia Minor at the end of the first century. So in an analysis of the discourses in the Gospel of John we come up against the same thing again and again: sayings of Jesus from the earlier tradition are elaborated, after the fashion of a Midrash, into homilies which take the form of a prose hymn. To a lesser degree this is also true of the synoptic gospels; they too have retrospective features, and do not disguise the fact that they were written in a post-Easter situation. These considerations have led to a considerable degree of scepticism; scholars doubt whether we are in a position to get back to the *ipsissima vox Jesu* and consequently are resigned to the position that the gospels give us the 'kerygma'—'didache' would probably be a better word!—of the primitive church. We shall attempt to show that this scepticism towards the historical evidence is unjustified by pointing to two linguistic characteristics of the *ipsissima vox Jesu*.

I

According to the unanimous testimony of the four gospels, Jesus *at all times*—with the sole exception of Mark 15.34 par. Matt. 27.46, which is a quotation from the Old Testament—addressed God as 'Father'.[1] Jesus almost always used this address 'Father' without any addition; the only passages in which an

---

* From: *Synoptische Studien Alfred Wikenhauser zum siebzigsten Geburtstag dargebracht*, Munich 1954, pp. 86-93 (*Abba*, Göttingen 1966, pp. 145-52). Details from the first section of this article are incorporated in the first essay of the present collection.

[1] Mark 14.36 (par. Matt. 26.39; Luke 22.42); Matt. 11.25, 26 (par. Luke 10.21 (*bis*)); Matt. 26.42; Luke 23.34, 46; John 11.41; 12.27, 28; 17.1, 5, 11, 21, 24, 25. All five strata of the gospel tradition (Mark, Logia, special Matthaean material, special Lucan material, John) agree here.

epithet appears alongside it are Matt. 11.25 (par. Luke 10.21) κύριε τοῦ οὐρανοῦ καὶ τῆς γῆς, and John 17.11 ἅγιε, 17.25 δίκαιε.[2] Mark 14.36 explicitly attests that in so doing he used the Aramaic vocative אַבָּא, and this is confirmed by the echo of the primitive church (Rom. 8.15; Gal. 4.6).[3] This *abba* ('my father') is not, as is frequently but erroneously asserted, a determinative form (= 'the father') which also represented the form with the pronominal suffix of the first person singular[4]; rather it is a vocative form, originally a piece of childish chatter, which then came to be used generally for the determinative form and the forms with the pronominal suffixes of the first person, although the memory of its humble origin was never lost.[5]

The result of a search for Jewish parallels to the use of *abba* as a form of address in prayers proves completely negative. As far as I can see, only three instances of the application of the Aramaic *abba* (without suffixes) to God can be found.[6]

1. In 1881, J. Levy drew attention to a variant to the *Targum on Job* 34.36, which occurs in a manuscript of the Bible, with Targum, written in the year 1238.[7] Whereas the editions of the

---

[2] The Lord's Prayer (Luke 11.2: πάτερ without any addition, cf. Matt. 6.9: πάτερ ἡμῶν ὁ ἐν τοῖς οὐρανοῖς) is relevant only as a supplement to our investigations, as it is a prayer for the disciples.

[3] A further confirmation is the occasional rendering of Jesus' address to God as ὁ πατήρ (Mark 14.36, cf. Matt. 11.26; Luke 10. 21; without the article: John 17.11 *v.l.*, 21 *v.l.*, 24 *v.l.*, 25 *v.l.*). This absolute vocative ὁ πατήρ has no connection with the replacement of the vocative with the nominative (with the article) in Attic Greek; it is a rendering of the Aramaic vocative *abba*, wrongly understood as a determinative form. This is clear (*a*) from the fact that the Attic idiom is limited to remarks addressed to underlings (Blass-Debrunner-Funk, §147.3), (*b*) from Mark 14.36; Rom. 8.15; Gal. 4.6: ἀββὰ ὁ πατήρ, and (*c*) from the absence of the absolute vocative ὁ πατήρ in the LXX, which did not find *abba* in the Hebrew or Aramaic original.

[4] Thus G. Kittel, ἀββᾶ, *TWNT* I (1933), p. 4. This assertion has often been repeated without it being noted that Kittel himself corrected it, a very short while afterwards, in fact in 1932, in: *Die Religionsgeschichte und das Urchristentum*, Gütersloh n.d., p. 146, n. 214.

[5] See above, pp. 58f. I have abandoned the view expressed in the first edition of this article in German, that the vocative form *abba* has arisen through a contraction of the diminutive form *abbāi, as suggested by G. Dalman, *Grammatik des jüdisch-palästinischen Aramäisch*[2], Leipzig 1905 = Darmstadt 1960, 9 §14.7d and f, pp. 90f.

[6] Apart from *Targ. Ps.* 89.27 (אבא את) and *Targ. Mal.* 2.10 (אבא חד לכלנא). In both these passages the Hebrew text determined the choice of wording.

[7] *Chaldäisches Wörterbuch über die Targumim*[3], Leipzig 1881, p. 1b. Levy's reference was taken up by Billerbeck II, p. 50, who is followed by G. Kittel, ἀββᾶ, p. 5.

Targum[8] read: צבינא דיתבחר איוב ('I wanted Job to be proved'), the MS of 1238 reads: רעינא פון דאבא דבשמיא יבחן איוב ('I longed for my Father in heaven to prove Job'). This isolated, late addition cannot possibly be the original text of the Targum to Job 34.36.

2. In 1898, G. Dalman drew attention to a second instance.[9] Referring to theH adrianic persecution, *Lev. R.* 32 on 24.10 says: 'Why will you be scourged? על שעשיתי רצון אבא שבשמים (because I have done the will of my heavenly Father).' But a comparison with the parallels shows that this instance too is a later addition to the text of the tradition. The passage does not occur in the earlier parallel *Mek. Ex.* 20.6.[10]

3. Far more important than these two late additions to the text is a third instance of the application of *abba* to God, which was pointed out by J. Leipoldt in 1941.[11] Its greater importance lies already in the fact that it contains the word *abba* without any addition—the two passages we have just discussed have the liturgical phrase 'Father in heaven'. But above all, it is particularly significant because of its age: it takes us into the first century BC. It is a story which is told of a grandson of Onias the Circle-maker, who was famous for his successful prayers for rain. Onias was a contemporary of the scholar Simeon b. Shaṭaḥ, who lived during the reigns of King Alexander Jannaeus (104-76 BC) and Queen Salome Alexandra (76-67 BC). He was killed in 65 BC, as we know from Josephus.[12] His grandson must therefore have lived in the last decades of the first century BC. The text (*b. Ta'an.* 23b) runs[13]:

---

[8] *Venetian Rabbinic Bible* of the year 1568; P. de Lagarde, *Hagiographa Chaldaice*, Lipsiae 1873; *Bible with Targum*, Wilna 1893.

[9] *The Words of Jesus*, I, ET, Edinburgh 1902, p. 188; G. Kittel, ἀββᾶ, p. 5.

[10] *Midr. Tehillim* 12.5 has the addition, but with 'abbi instead of *abba*.—For the sake of completeness it should be noted that G. Dalman, *Die Worte Jesu*, I[1, 2], pp. 152-4, also adduces a number of examples of the religious use of *abba* with suffixes: אבוהון די (*Midr. Abba Gorion* 1.1); אבוהון דבשמיא (Midr. Abba Gorion 1.1); אבוהי דשמיא (*j. Ma'as.* 3.50c. 11); לאבוכון דבשמיא בשמיא (*Kaddish*); (Aramaic Haggadah for the feast of Pentecost). In each case God is distinguished from an earthly father as the father 'in heaven' or by other additions. Examples from the Targum in Billerbeck I, pp. 395f.; these instances from the Targum can be increased, cf. G. Dalman, *Die Worte Jesu* I[2], pp. 296-304, passim. Only in the two passages mentioned in n. 6, however, do we have the form *abba* (without a suffix) with which we are exclusively concerned.

[11] *Jesu Verhältnis zu Juden und Griechen*, Leipzig 1941, pp. 136f.

[12] *Antt.* 14.22-24.

[13] According to the 1721 Frankfurt edition of the Babylonian Talmud.

'Hanin ha-Nehba was the son of the daughter of Onias the Circle-maker. When the world needed rain, our teachers used to send schoolchildren to him, who seized the hem of his coat[14] and implored him: "*Abba, abba, habb lan miṭra* (Daddy, daddy, give us rain)." He said to Him (God): "Master of the world, grant it (the rain) for the sake of these who are not yet able to distinguish between an *abba* who has the power to give rain and an *abba* who has not." '

Here God is designated by Hanin as *abba* in a quite unliturgical way. Note, however, that he is simply repeating what the children say! Hanin is appealing to God's mercy by taking up the '*abba, abba*' of the school children and describing God as the '*abba* who has the power to give rain'.

This exhausts the evidence for the application of *abba* (without a suffix) to God, and so we can go on to draw the conclusion. *There is not a single example of the use of* abba (*without a suffix*) *as an address to God in the whole of Jewish literature*. God is not addressed as *abba* in any of the three passages we have discussed. The reason for this has been recognized by G. Dalman[15] and T. Zahn,[16] and the final passage, discussed above, from *b. Ta'an.* 23b confirms their judgment: *abba* is familiar language.[17] *Abba* ('my father') is in fact derived from the chatter of children.[18] When a child has begun to 'eat bread' (i.e. soon after it has been weaned) it learns to say *abba* and *imma*.[19] Although *abba* was no longer restricted to children's talk in Jesus' time, it nevertheless remained a familiar word with which no-one would have dared to address God. *No Jew ever called God* abba, *yet the evangelists record that Jesus always called God* abba, '*my Father*' (except for the cry from the cross, Mark 15.34). We have thus established the emergence of a completely new manner of speaking which at the same time

[14] A gesture of urgent supplication, cf. Mark 5.27.

[15] *The Words of Jesus*, I, *ET*, Edinburgh 1902, pp. 191f.

[16] T. Zahn-F. Hauck, *Der Brief des Paulus an die Römer*[3], Leipzig-Erlangen 1925, p. 396, n. 93.

[17] T. Zahn (see preceding note) pointed out that the church fathers Chrysostom, Theodore and Theodoret, who were brought up in Antioch probably under the supervision of Syriac speaking nurses and nursery-maids, unanimously bear witness that small children used to address their fathers as '*abba*'. G. Kittel, ἀββᾶ, p. 5, deserves credit for indicating the importance of this statement.   [18] More details above, n. 5.

[19] *b. Ber.* 40a; *b. Sanh.* 70b (G. Dalman, *Die Worte Jesu* I[2], Leipzig 1930, p. 302).

reflects a most profound new relationship with God. We cannot be sure of the authenticity of each of the 15 passages[20] in which it occurs, but the address itself is without question an incontestable characteristic of the *ipsissima vox Jesu*.

2

It has been pointed out almost *ad nauseam*[21] that a new use of the word *amen* emerges in the four gospels *which is without analogy in the whole of Jewish literature and in the rest of the New Testament.* Whereas according to idiomatic Jewish usage the word *amen* is used to affirm, endorse or appropriate the words of another person,[22] in the tradition of the saying of Jesus it is used *without exception* to introduce and endorse Jesus' own words. The formula is always ἀμὴν λέγω ὑμῖν (σοι) in the Synoptics, and ἀμὴν, ἀμὴν λέγω ὑμῖν (σοι) in John. There are 13 instances in Mark, 30 in Matthew (+ 18.19 *v.l.*), 6 in Luke and 25 in John. *So we have a completely new manner of speaking, strictly limited to the gospels and here again limited to the sayings of Jesus.* Here the *amen* serves to replace oath-like formulae of asseveration which Jesus forbids in Matt. 5.33-37 because they are a misuse of the divine name; it is even more likely that the formula *amen* should be seen as an alternative to the authoritative prophetic formula 'Thus says the Lord', which avoids using the divine name.[23]

The only question is whether it is probable that on occasion the tradition has introduced this *amen* into the sayings of Jesus. After all, Matthew has the phrase twice where it does not occur in the Marcan parallel (Matt. 19.23; 24.2), and the 25 Johannine passages indicate that it was used as a formula in the tradition of the primitive church. But the Gospel of John can be passed over for the moment, as the doubling of the *amen*, which is always

[20] 19 instances including parallels (see n. 1). They are examined in 'Abba', above, pp. 54-63.

[21] G. Dalman, *The Words of Jesus*, I, ET, Edinburgh 1902, pp. 226-9, with Appendix to *Die Worte Jesu*, I², Leipzig 1930, p. 383; *id.*, *Jesus-Jeshua*, London 1929, p. 30; Billerbeck I, pp. 242-4; A. Schlatter, *Der Evangelist Matthäus*, Stuttgart 1929 = ⁶1963, p. 155; H. Schlier, ἀμήν, *TWNT* I (1933), pp. 339-42.

[22] Even Jer. 28.6: 'And the prophet Jeremiah said, "Amen! May the Lord do so"', is no exception. The *amen* is not prefixed to strengthen Jeremiah's own remarks: it is his answer to the previous words of the prophet Hananiah of Gibeon. The same is true of *Soṭah* 2.5. 'To end one's own prayer with *āmēn* was considered to be a sign of ignorance' (G. Dalman, *Jesus-Jeshua*, ibid.).

[23] T. W. Manson, *The Teaching of Jesus²*, Cambridge 1935 = 1948, p. 207.

strictly observed, is a special usage there. In the synoptic tradition, on the contrary, we notice an increasing tendency to delete the phrase with *amen* or to translate it. This tendency has already begun with Mark, as can be seen from a comparison of Mark 6.4 with Luke 4.24 (+ ἀμὴν λέγω ὑμῖν).²⁴ The tendency is even stronger in Matthew: the words λέγω ὑμῖν (σοι) are kept, but ἀμήν is translated ναί²⁵ or replaced by πλήν,²⁶ διὰ τοῦτο²⁷ and δέ²⁸; three times a simple καί takes the place of the whole phrase ἀμὴν λέγω ὑμῖν.²⁹ Luke goes even further. He has only kept the phrase with *amen* six times (three times in the Marcan material³⁰ and three times in his special material³¹); he translates ἀμήν with ναί,³² ἀληθῶς,³³ ἐπ’ ἀληθείας,³⁴ replaces it with γάρ³⁵ or omits it³⁶; the whole phrase ἀμὴν λέγω ὑμῖν is repeatedly replaced by a simple καί,³⁷ δέ,³⁸ πλήν,³⁹ or πλὴν ἰδού,⁴⁰ or completely omitted.⁴¹ In view of this, it becomes an urgent question whether in a whole series of synoptic λέγω ὑμῖν (σοι) passages an original ἀμήν has not fallen out or been replaced, although there are no parallels with ἀμήν to support such a suggestion; most of the passages occur in special material, i.e. sayings for which we have no parallels to serve as comparisons.⁴² Only in John do we have a movement in the opposite direction, where the formula with a double *amen*, which has an almost

---

²⁴ In view of Luke’s avoidance of ἀμήν it is extremely unlikely that the ἀμήν in Luke 4.24 is an addition.

²⁵ Matt. 11.9.   ²⁶ 11.22, 24 (cf. 10.15; 26.64).

²⁷ 12.31 (cf. Mark 3.28).   ²⁸ 26.29 (cf. Mark 14.25).

²⁹ 12.32 (cf. Mark 3.28); 12.39; 16.4 (cf. Mark 8.12).

³⁰ 18.17, 29; 21.32.   ³¹ See below, n. 43.

³² Luke 7.26; 11.51 (cf. Matt. 23.36); 12.5.

³³ 9.27 (cf. Mark 9.1); 12.44 (cf. Matt. 24.47); 21.3 (cf. Mark 12.43).

³⁴ 4.25 (cf. v. 24).   ³⁵ 22.16, 18 (cf. Mark 14.25).

³⁶ 7.9 (cf. Matt. 8.10); 7.28 (cf. Matt. 11.11); 10.12 (cf. Matt. 10.15); 10.24 (cf. Matt. 13.17); 12.59 (cf. Matt. 5.26); 15.7, 10 (cf. Matt. 18.13); 22.34 (cf. Mark 14.30).

³⁷ 11.29 (cf. Mark 8.12); 12.10 (cf. Mark 3.28).

³⁸ 16.17 (cf. Matt. 5.18); 22.28 (cf. Matt. 19.28).

³⁹ 10.14 (cf. Matt. 10.15).   ⁴⁰ 22.21 (cf. Mark 14.18).

⁴¹ 13.25 (cf. Matt. 25.12); 17.6 (cf. Matt. 17.20).

⁴² The following passages are relevant, though it is impossible to come to a decision in each individual case: Mark: 9.13; 11.24 (cf. v. 23!). Matt.: 5.20; 6.25, 29; 8.11; 12.6, 36; 16.18; 17.12; 18.10; 19.9; (21.43); 23.39. Luke: 7.47; 11.8, 9; 12.4 (cf. v.5!), 8, 22, 27; 13.24, 35; 14.24; 16.9; 17.34; 18.8, 14; 19.26, 40; 22.37. In particular, the endings of the Lucan parables with λέγω ὑμῖν (Luke 11.8; 13.24; 14.24; 15.7, 10; 18.8, 14; 19.26) should be compared with the ἀμὴν λέγω ὑμῖν (σοι) of the Matthaean endings (Matt. 5.26; 21.31; 25.12; cf. 25.40, 45); it is probable that Matthew has the older tradition here because the simple λέγω ὑμῖν is a characteristic of Luke.

liturgical ring, now begins to occupy a considerable place. As the primitive church retained the Jewish custom of endorsing the words of a spokesman with *amen* in its services[43] and increasingly eliminated the *amen* from the tradition of the sayings of Jesus in the decades after it had moved into a Hellenistic milieu, we may conclude that *amen* has been introduced only in isolated instances.[44]

An examination of the thirteen ἀμὴν λέγω ὑμῖν (σοι) sayings in the Gospel of Mark confirms this conclusion; without exception they show signs of primitiveness, e.g. in their emphatic eschatology and the sharpness of the opposition to the Pharisees.

3.28: The unforgiveable sin
8.12: The refusal of signs
9.1:   Some of those standing here will not die before the parousia
9.41: The cup of cold water
10.15: Only the childlike will enter the kingdom
10.29: The hundredfold recompense
11.23: Faith that will move mountains
12.43: The poor widow made the greatest sacrifice
13.30: This γενεά will not pass away until all is fulfilled
14.9: In the final judgment the act of the woman will be mentioned before God's throne, so that God will remember her graciously[45]
14.18: One of you will betray me
14.25: The avowal of abstinence[46]
14.30: The prophecy of Peter's denial

The 18 *amen* sayings which occur in Matthaean saying-material which is not included in Mark give equal signs of being primitive: 5.18 (probably to be related to the prophecies, particularly the

[43] I Cor. 14.16; II Cor. 1.20; Rev. 5.14; 7.12; 19.4; Justin, *Apol.* I 65.3; 67.5. The strength of the influence of the liturgical heritage can be illustrated from a single remark. The church's decorated Amen derives from the liturgy of the Synagogue, which had the following rule: 'If a man lengthens the *amen*, his lifetime will be lengthened (by God)' (*b. Ber.* 47a, saying of Ben Azzai, *c.* AD 110).

[44] Perhaps Matt. 19.23; 24.2 (see above).

[45] For a justification of this interpretation of the passage see my article on 'Mc 14.9', *ZNW* 44 (1952-3), pp. 103-7 (revised version in *Abba*, pp. 115-20).

[46] Cf. J. Jeremias, *The Eucharistic Words of Jesus*, ET², London 1966, pp. 207-18 ('Jesus' avowal of abstinence').

prophecies of suffering in the Old Testament); 5.26; 6.2, 5, 16; 8.10; 10.15, 23; 11.11; 13.17; 18.13, 18; 21.31; 23.36; 24.47; 25.12, 40, 45.[47]

So in the *amen* sayings, too, we have the emergence of a new and completely unique manner of speaking. And once again, the new form is matched by a new content. Here is a consciousness of rank which lays claim to divine authority. Once again, we have here without question an incontestable linguistic characteristic of the *ipsissima vox Jesu*.

3

In conclusion, here are a few further peculiarities of the gospel tradition which may be regarded as characteristics of the way Jesus spoke, both because they appear to the same degree in different strata of tradition and because they are unique (or far more frequent) in comparison with contemporary sources: the parables,[48] the character of Jesus' use of rhythm (four-stresses for the instruction of the disciples, three-stresses to mark particular sentences in Jesus' preaching, the Kinah metre [3 + 2] for strongly emotive sayings)[49] and the periphrasis of the divine name with the passive, which occurs strikingly often. Both antithetic parallelism[50] and also, probably, the tripartite structure of sayings[51] call for closer investigation in this direction, in comparison with the literature of the time.

[47] It is not clear whether we should count Matt. 19.28 as a nineteenth saying, because the ἀμὴν λέγω ὑμῖν here could come from Mark 10.29; Matt. 18.19 could be counted as a twentieth if the reading + ἀμήν is regarded as original. —There are only three *amen* sayings in the Lucan special material: 4.24; 12.37; 23.43.

[48] J. Jeremias, *The Parables of Jesus*, ET², London 1963, pp. 11f.

[49] C. F. Burney, *The Poetry of Our Lord*, Oxford 1925, pp. 100-46.

[50] *Ibid.*, pp. 71-88. This eminent specialist concludes that in antithetic parallelism like Matt. 10.39, we have the *ipsissima verba* of Jesus 'more nearly than in any sentence otherwise expressed' (p. 84).

[51] J. Jeremias, *Jesus als Weltvollender* (BFCT 33.4), Gütersloh 1930, p. 21, n. 1 (the list simply contains instances from a far greater range of material; Mark 2.18-22 should be deleted).

INDEXES

INDEX OF MODERN AUTHORS

INDEX OF BIBLICAL REFERENCES